ADVANCE PRAISE FOR

Rescued

"Rescue a dog, and the dog will rescue you. I can vouch for that, and Peter Zheutlin does a lovely, moving job of exploring the subject. *Rescued* is a delightful read."

—Dean Koontz, *New York Times* bestselling author

"*Rescued* is a must-read for anyone who has ever experienced the love of a dog. Peter Zheutlin does a masterful job conveying the meaning and joy that come from helping a once-homeless animal feel secure, loved, and part of the family. This beautiful book belongs on every dog lover's shelf."

—Laura T. Coffey, bestselling author of
My Old Dog: Rescued Pets with Remarkable Second Acts

"I loved this book. It eloquently describes the singular joy of giving a rescue dog one's hearth and heart."

—Lisa Mullins, anchor at WBUR, Boston

"*Rescued* is a wide-ranging and intensely moving meditation on sharing one's life with adopted dogs. Peter Zheutlin is one of the few journalists who has taken on the complex world of animal rescue and actually gotten it right."

—Bronwen Dickey, author of
Pit Bull: The Battle over an American Icon

"In *Rescued*, Peter shows us that shelter dogs are some of our greatest teachers. Stories about rescue become tales of personal growth, where dogs are given second chances and people are reminded that our best lives are lived when we open our arms to those that need us."

—Jesse Freidin, photographer and author of *Finding Shelter*

Rescued

Also by Peter Zheutlin

RESCUE ROAD:
One Man, Thirty Thousand Dogs, and
a Million Miles on the Last Hope Highway

AROUND THE WORLD ON TWO WHEELS:
Annie Londonderry's Extraordinary Ride

Rescued

*What Second-Chance Dogs Teach Us
About Living with Purpose, Loving
with Abandon, and Finding Joy
in the Little Things*

Peter Zheutlin

A TARCHERPERIGEE BOOK

An imprint of Penguin Random House LLC
375 Hudson Street
New York, New York 10014

First edition 2017

Poem on p. 169 by Joanne Sebring

TarcherPerigee with tp colophon is a registered trademark of
Penguin Random House LLC.

Most TarcherPerigee books are available at special quantity discounts
for bulk purchase for sales promotions, premiums, fund-raising, and
educational needs. Special books or book excerpts also
can be created to fit specific needs. For details, write:
SpecialMarkets@penguinrandomhouse.com.

LIBRARY OF CONGRESS CATALOGING-IN-PUBLICATION DATA
Names: Zheutlin, Peter, author
Title: Rescued: what second-chance dogs teach us about living with
purpose, loving with abandon, and finding joy in the little things /
Peter Zheutlin.
Description: First edition. | New York, New York: TarcherPerigee, 2017.
Identifiers: LCCN 2017016377 | ISBN 9780143131175
Subjects: LCSH: Dogs. | Dog rescue. | Human-aninal relationships.
Classification: LCC SF426 .Z44 2017 | DDC 636.73—dc23 LC record
available at https://lccn.loc.gov/2017016377

Printed in the United States of America
1   3   5   7   9   10   8   6   4   2

BOOK DESIGN BY KATY RIEGEL

For my wonderful wife, Judy.

For more than twenty years I rebuffed

all her efforts to convince me we should

have a dog. Nevertheless, she persisted,

and I'm glad she did.

CONTENTS

Amazing grace, how sweet the sound

That saved a wretch like me.

I once was lost but now I'm found.

Was blind but now I see.

—JOHN NEWTON

Salina and Albie

INTRODUCTION

*Dogs are our link to paradise. They don't know evil or
jealousy or discontent. To sit with a dog on a hillside on
a glorious afternoon is to be back in Eden, where doing
nothing was not boring—it was peace.*
                                                  —MILAN KUNDERA

I N THE EARLY FALL OF 2012, after he'd been with us
nearly four months, our rescue dog Albie and I
walked the pine-needle-covered trails of what was fast
becoming our special place: Elm Bank along the Charles
River, a forested preserve outside Boston. The October
air smelled of earth and woody decay, the light was bril-
liant and sharp, and leaves of red and gold floated gently
downward on imperceptible air currents until they came
to rest softly on the ground.

It was Albie's first New England fall. He was, the vet
surmised, about two or three years old, and he was one
very lucky dog. Picked up as stray in Deville, Louisiana,
the previous February, he had languished for five
months in a "high-kill" shelter where nine out of every

ten dogs that enter never leave.* Albie was an underdog in every sense; one of the countless unwanted and
unknown dogs that fill shelters throughout the South.
With no one looking for him and no place to go, he was
on death row with slim chances of survival. But thanks
to a shelter volunteer who took a shine to him, he de-
fied those odds and was accepted into an adoption program run by Labs4rescue, a Connecticut-based rescue
organization. We saw Albie's profile on their Web site,
fell in love with him through some photographs and a
short video, and in early July he came north on a rescue
dog transport called Rescue Road Trips to join our
family.

We knew from our Labs4rescue adoption coordinator, Keri Toth, that Albie had been in a concrete-and-
chain-link enclosure for nearly five months in a
Louisiana shelter, but we didn't know—no one knew—
how he'd come to be wandering alone, malnourished,
and frightened. So, from the moment he landed in our
arms, we vowed to do everything humanly possible to
give him a wonderful life, free from fear and hunger and
want. We knew nothing of his previous life—whether
he'd been abandoned, neglected, or abused, or was simply lost—but it was, in part, the mystery of his life before
that bound us so tightly to him. We couldn't know what

---

*There's no precise definition of a "high-kill" shelter, but the term refers to
shelters where a high percentage of dogs are put down rather than adopted out
or returned to owners who reclaim them.

wrongs and misfortunes had befallen him. But we were determined to right them anyway.

ALBIE IS A YELLOW LAB and golden retriever mix—at least that's everyone's best guess, because you can't really tell a dog's entire genetic heritage based on looks alone. By the time of our walk in the woods that golden October day Albie had gained some weight; he was up to about seventy-five pounds from sixty-five, and I was now able to trust he would return when called if I let him off-leash. He'd spy something, or smell something, then race off into the woods with astonishing agility, leaping over fallen trees and bounding through the dry underbrush. His fur, a yellowish wheat color, blended perfectly with the surroundings. At first, whenever he disappeared for more than a minute or two, I'd get frantic and start calling for him, convinced he was gone for good. But as someone said to me once in those same woods about Albie, "You may not know where he is, but he always knows where you are." I eventually came to trust those words, too.

After he'd been gone, sometimes for several minutes, he'd reappear on the trail, perhaps a hundred yards ahead, then come racing toward me with a smile and, it seemed, proud of himself. One of Albie's most endearing physical traits is a nose that at certain times of the year turns the color of a pencil eraser. (It's called "snow nose" because the color tends to lighten as winter approaches.) He'd stare up at me with those deep brown pools he has for eyes, his eraser nose twitching, hoping for a treat, and all I could think was that this was the most earnest dog I'd ever met. We were buddies.

On our autumn walks through those woods, which we made almost daily, I often felt an intense sense of well-being. Albie exuded the energy of a puppy. He was, after all, still young. I, on the other hand, was about to turn fifty-nine. Not so young anymore. And it struck me: over the years to come, Albie would start gaining on me, because dogs age faster than humans. (The canard that one human year equals seven dog years isn't quite true, but it suffices here.) By the time I would be undeniably on the brink of old age, so, too, would Albie. We were going to grow old together. I was teaching Albie to love and to trust and to live in a family. Little did I know that he would wind up teaching me far more.

As HUMANS, we love to tell our personal stories about our relationships with our canine companions. From John Steinbeck's *Travels with Charley* to John Grogan's *Marley & Me* and beyond, books about people and their dogs abound. Many concern dogs who have saved their people, pulling them through health crises, depression, divorces, or the deaths of loved ones, or changing life for their afflicted children.

This is not one of those books.

I had my cancer scare in 2003, well before Albie was born. My wife, Judy, and I are happily married going on nearly thirty years. We have our struggles, as every couple and every family do, and while Albie is always a comfort in tough times he hasn't saved us from calamity or existential crisis. Unless something unexpected happens while this book is in progress, it will have a happy ending, with Albie and me still walking the familiar trails we love so much. We'll just be a bit farther down the road, so to speak.

So, no, this is not a book about someone who rescued a dog only to realize the dog rescued them, a cliché I've grown slightly weary of even though I'm very devoted to the rescue dog movement. Don't get me wrong. Many of the books that do take this approach are wonderful reads. But judging by the countless "Who Rescued Who?" bumper stickers I see on high-end SUVs every day, there are an inordinate number of well-heeled suburbanites who were once in need of salvation.

This isn't to say dogs don't transform lives. They most surely do. And it isn't to say dogs can't turn lives around or help people heal. They most certainly can, and we'll see some examples of that in this book. Albie has added so much to my life, to *our* lives, and he has, in many ways, transformed it—after all, he turned me into a "dog person." But I can't say he rescued me, or Judy, or made me a better person, though he brings out the best in me. He makes me laugh and he's made me cry, he makes me smile (a lot) and he's made me mad (very, very rarely). Mostly he just makes my heart leap. He's also taught me a thing or two, about life, about love, and about what it means to give a true underdog a second chance.

> The lessons that rescue dogs can teach us go beyond simply improving our interactions with them. They touch us in far deeper ways that can change our human relationships, our habits, our mind-sets, and our lives for the better.

Albie's not the smartest dog, or the best-behaved; not the least obtrusive, and far from the least neurotic. But when he wakes me up in the morning with his low grumble and my eyes crack open, barely, to see his big nose about two inches from mine, I know it's going to be a good day, or at least a better day than it would have been without him. When I pull in the driveway and he's waiting at the front door, as he almost always is, I feel valued. And on the nights when he curls up next to me in bed I am grateful to be with him and to know he's had another day when he's been loved and well fed and kept safe; in other words, another day in a place we call *home*.

This, then, is a book about walking into the autumn of my own life alongside a very lucky, slightly goofy, and impossibly earnest dog—and eventually a second rescue dog named Salina—and what I've learned along the way. And because I have met or talked with many, many people about their rescue dogs, it draws on their experiences, too, and the universal wisdom they've gleaned from living with and loving a second-chance dog. Some of it is prosaic, some of it is subtle, but some, I think, is profound. The lessons that rescue dogs can teach us go well beyond simply improving our interactions with them. They touch us in far deeper ways that can change our human relationships, our habits, our mind-sets, and our lives for the better. So I've endeavored to share some of this happily learned wisdom here.

Last but not least, this is also a book about unconditional two-way love, a love much simpler and unadorned than the love between two people. It is, after all, much easier when only one of you can talk.

Rescued

Noah and Sadie

CHAPTER ONE

Saving Albie

*A dog is the only thing on earth that loves you more
than he loves himself.*   —JOSH BILLINGS

A T THE VERY END of *Annie Hall*, the Oscar-winning
Best Picture in 1978, the main character, Alvy,
played by Woody Allen, crosses paths again with Annie
on the Upper West Side. They had loved and laughed
and struggled, but their romance was star-crossed and
ended with heartache. After an awkward but tender ex-
change they say good-bye once again, and we hear a
voice-over spoken by Alvy as he watches Annie melt
away into the depths of Manhattan.

"After that it got pretty late," Alvy says. "And we
both hadda go, but it was great seeing Annie again,
right? I realized what a terrific person she was and—and
how much fun it was just knowing her and I—I thought
of that old joke, you know, this—this—this guy goes to
a psychiatrist and says, 'Doc, uh, my brother's crazy. He

thinks he's a chicken.' And, uh, the doctor says, 'Well, why don't you turn him in?' And the guy says, 'I would, but I need the eggs.' Well, I guess that's pretty much how I feel about relationships. You know, they're totally irrational and crazy and absurd and . . . but, uh, I guess we keep goin' through it because, uh, most of us need the eggs."

That small monologue goes a long way toward explaining why, just as Judy and I were about to become empty nesters, I finally agreed to adopt a rescue dog. I needed the eggs. Let me explain.

Albie is one of many thousands of "rescue dogs" that are part of a great migration of shelter and street dogs that make their way primarily from southern states (and the Caribbean) to "forever" homes, mainly in the Northeast, every year, a migration facilitated by legions of tireless, bighearted people devoted to saving as many dogs as possible. I wrote about one such group of people in my last book, *Rescue Road: One Man, Thirty Thousand Dogs, and a Million Miles on the Last Hope Highway.**

The "one man" of the subtitle is Greg Mahle of Zanesville, Ohio, who, over more than a decade, has logged more than a million weary miles in a tractor-trailer to deliver dogs like Albie from the mean streets and high-kill shelters of the Deep South and into the

---

*If you have read *Rescue Road*, you will find the basic outline of Albie's story familiar. But some of it bears repeating here to provide context, especially since not everyone reading this book will also have read *Rescue Road*.

arms of loving families. But for every lucky dog that gets that ride to freedom, countless others perish. The canine overpopulation problem is vast—there are over a million strays living on the streets of Houston alone.

I knew nothing of this when we decided to adopt a rescue dog, not the size of the problem or anything about the networks of people working to save them. All I knew was that, based on some photographs, a short video, and a conversation with Keri Toth, Albie's adoption coordinator with Connecticut-based Labs4rescue, we had committed to giving Albie a home, a *forever* home. In fact, it came as a surprise when I learned Albie wasn't in Connecticut and that we couldn't just drive down from Boston and pick him up the next day. We had to wait a couple of weeks until Keri, who is based in Alexandria, Louisiana, and where Albie had been in a high-kill shelter for five months, could get him on Greg Mahle's truck.

Since we were already in love from watching his little video over and over, the days passed slowly. Even when he reached Massachusetts we had to wait two additional days because the state requires rescue dogs coming from out of state to be quarantined for forty-eight hours and reexamined by a veterinarian before they are released. Even though every dog coming into the state has to have an interstate health certificate signed by a veterinarian in the state of origin, the state insists on the quarantine.

What could Albie have been making of it all? He

went from wandering alone on a deserted country road to a cell-like enclosure in a noisy shelter for five months, into a kennel on a big truck with no clue where he was going, and, once again, into another shelter, only to be picked up two days later by a family he'd never met but with whom he would spend the rest of his life.

Judy had wanted a dog since before we had kids. And when we had kids they, too, of course, wanted a dog. But I was steadfast. I knew, despite the promises, that the lion's share of the work, especially early morning walks on subzero mornings across sheets of ice so a dog could poop, would be *my* job. Judy isn't exactly what you'd call a diligent housekeeper, so I knew it would also fall mostly on me to vacuum up the shed fur, wipe off the muddy paws, and pick up the dog toys strewn about the house. When our boys were little and keeping the house in order was a full-time job, it was *my* job: I changed sheets, vacuumed carpets, organized toys over and over and over, pulled Legos out of toilets, and generally tried to keep the house from descending into utter chaos.

My resistance to a dog started to crack, however, when our friends Anne Marie and Dave asked if we could take care of Reilly, their black Lab, for a weekend. That's the official version, anyway. What really happened was that Judy conspired with Anne Marie to have us host Reilly, the first step in a well-considered plan to soften me up for a dog of our own.

Reilly arrived, his signature red kerchief around his

neck, with a bag of food, a box of treats, and a very comfortable, well-worn bed. Labs are known for their high energy, but Reilly was very mellow; he had the slightly aloof but genial temperament and disposition of Alistair Cooke, who for years hosted *Masterpiece Theatre* on PBS. I felt like I was going to have to prove myself worthy of being his host, not the other way around.

So for two days Reilly occasionally chased a tennis ball (sometimes I had the feeling he'd rather be playing bridge), gazed with a pitiful look on his face at every morsel of food I put in my mouth, and took leisurely walks around the lake at Wellesley College, where Judy and I took him to see if he might be interested in applying. The visit was such a success that we invited Reilly back, and back he came a couple of weeks later when Anne Marie and Dave went off to their son Liam's college graduation. This time, feeling very much at home, Reilly chilled in the TV room with us, took a few walks, and generally made himself part of the family. We were sad when it was time for him to go home. (Reilly died in 2015 at the age of fourteen. Dave and Anne Marie miss him terribly and we miss him, too. He became a friend of Albie's.)

By the time I relented a few weeks later, my older son, Danny, was in college and my younger son, Noah, was about to be a senior in high school. I didn't realize it then, but it was the prospect of being an empty nester that caused my implacable opposition to crumble.

All through my sons' childhoods I had worked at home because I didn't want the formative years to fly by and not be an integral part of them. Now, before I knew it, it was going to be just Judy and me, alone together in a house that had once bustled with the activities of toddlers, then children, and then teenagers. Some couples find that once the kids are gone, so, too, is the glue that held them together. I wasn't worried about that: Judy and I have plenty to talk about, though each of us occasionally feels as if we're talking to the wall, which is no doubt how she felt during the twenty-plus years she tried to persuade me to get a dog. But I worried that having a dog would mean that we wouldn't have the unfettered freedom that would come with being empty nesters. And I was concerned that, at nine years Judy's senior, I might run out of gas while a dog was still at the peak of its doggy energy. Yet, I also had a feeling that we stood to gain more than we had to lose.

MY OWN FATHER had been a work-at-home dad of sorts, and that experience shaped my own plans for parenthood. He was a pediatrician and for most of my growing up his office was in a converted garage attached to our house. A small half bath connected the house to the office. It meant that my brother Michael and I saw our dad all the time; he wasn't commuting to a distant office we could hardly imagine, doing work we couldn't comprehend. We knew it was his job to take care of kids just like us. He'd walk through that bathroom portal many times a day and change, magically it seemed, from Dr. Zheutlin to our dad and back again like a medical version of Clark Kent, and I did in fact come to see him as a superhero. Occasionally I'd come home from school and find the house door locked, so I'd go in through the office and see my father, tall, trim, and handsome, stethoscope around his neck, a calm, commanding figure amid the chaos of crying children and worried mothers (and it always seemed to be mothers).

One day, when I was about seven, I heard a scream and looked out my bedroom window, which was above the office entrance. A mother carrying a small child came running up the driveway and into the office. Almost immediately the front doorbell rang and I rushed to answer it because my mother wasn't home. A policeman holding an oxygen tank asked where the office was and I directed him through the house to the office. I knew something terrible was happening just beyond that little bathroom door.

About fifteen minutes later, or maybe longer (it's impossible to know more than half a century on), I found my dad in the dining room pouring a glass of whiskey. It wasn't for him, he explained. It was for a young mother sitting in his office whose child had just died. I have to believe that was my father's darkest hour in a long career in which he was deeply loved by his patients, and to this day I think of his pouring that glass of whiskey as part of his very humane way of practicing medicine.

Had he worked in an office away from home there are so many things I never would have understood or appreciated about him. Maybe it was ego, but without being conscious of it, I wanted my kids to know me, too, even if I never did anything as heroic as my father. And I just didn't want to be the dad who rushed home to tuck his kids in at night and was running for the train before they were up for school the next morning.

While being a work-at-home dad was deeply gratifying, it did have some unintended consequences. A few years ago our boys confessed that when they were younger they were somewhat mystified by the fact that I was home all day while most fathers they knew went off to work. Yet there I was, walking them to and from school and playing catch with them on weekday afternoons. Since I had, according to them, "no visible means of support"—writing was not a "real" job, and their mom was a stay-at-home writer, too—the money we were living on had to come from somewhere. And they came to the rather arresting conclusion that we were Russian spies, a belief they apparently harbored, with more or less conviction, for several years.

It may not have helped that we had occasional Russian visitors, friends I had made during several trips to the Soviet Union, and later Russia, while working for an international peace organization in the late 1980s and early 1990s. And there were the Soviet-era propaganda posters I bought as souvenirs and hung in the basement. When the boys were young and started a lemonade stand I took one of those posters, one that featured Vladimir Lenin striking a heroic pose with one arm outstretched, and stapled a plastic cup to Lenin's hand. We branded the product "Leninade" and used it to attract passersby. No wonder the kids thought we were Russian spies.

BUT IT'S CLEAR TO ME NOW that I relented and agreed to get a dog because I wasn't done nurturing. I needed the eggs Woody Allen was talking about. The boys didn't need me to help them set up their lemonade stands anymore, or teach them to how to ride a bike, or read them a bedtime story. Those days and nights, especially the nights when sleep eluded the kids, could seem so long sometimes. But the years? Well, they'd passed in the proverbial blink of an eye. Thinking back on it, I hoped a dog would help stave off the inevitable slide into late midlife, defined not so much by chronological age but as the time when the kids leave home. I wasn't young anymore, no matter how fit and youthful I felt, but I wasn't ready to be old, either.

When we leave the freedom of our early years behind to raise children, we do it because it adds meaning to our lives; we know we will not survive—we all die someday— but by having children we draw comfort in knowing we will, barring tragedy, *be survived*. Our minuscule influence on this world will continue to ripple in some small way through our children and their children and their children. We take our place in the great continuum of life (or, to quote *The Lion King*, which I think I watched more than a hundred times when the kids were little, the "circle of life"). There are many ways to live a meaningful life with or without children, but for me having children gives my life purpose and meaning in the most fundamental way.

But why, with those children about take flight on their own, with the freedom once enjoyed in youth about to be restored, would anyone adopt a rescue dog and be tied once again to cleaning up poop, sleep and feeding schedules, vet (doctor's) appointments (and vet bills), dog (baby) sitters, messes, and wrestling with behavioral challenges? In the case of a rescue dog—a dog once destined, perhaps, to die alone and forgotten in a shelter—the answer is the same: *it gives life meaning*.

Just ask Andrea Stewart and Linda Zaleskie of Brooklyn, who adopted a hard-luck dog named Noah, abandoned on the streets of Houston.

When Melissa Melvin—a volunteer with Melrose Park Neglected Dogs, a rescue organization that works in the Melrose Park area of Houston—first came upon the dog that would come to be known as Noah, she thought he was dead. He was covered with insect and dog bites and scabs, his feet were swollen, and he was suffering from severe mange and starvation. He would later test positive for heartworm. It appeared Noah had been dumped there at some point in his short life—he was about a year or two—to endure one excruciating day after another.

Melissa approached Kathy Wetmore, the founder of Houston's Shaggy Dog Rescue, and she agreed to take Noah into her rescue. Several months of intensive veterinary care followed, more than $10,000 in all, most paid from Kathy's own pocket.

Today, Noah, a smallish Lab mix who still bears the scars of mange, is a happy, healthy dog living a good life in Brooklyn with Andrea and Linda, a married couple, and their other rescue dog, Sadie.

"I really thought Sadie would love having a sibling," Andrea told me. "She has so much energy! From the time we got her she was such a sweet girl and very responsive to commands. She listens and she's obedient."

"In the city one day she slipped her leash," added Linda. "Andrea just said, 'Sit,' and she sat. We were in SoHo and there was a lot of traffic but she sat. That she was so easy is what enabled us to think about a second dog."

"I was following Noah's progress on the Shaggy Dog Rescue Facebook page," said Andrea. "Kathy Wetmore had found a foster [temporary caretaker] who cared for him during his treatments, Stephanie Hitt, and she posted a lot of pictures of him and I just fell in love."

"We were worried about Sadie being relegated to a secondary position if we adopted another dog," Linda added. "She's far from submissive but I didn't want her steamrolled by another dog. So we asked Stephanie, who'd had Noah for six months and had many other dogs, a lot of pointed questions. She knew Noah well and had seen him interact with the other dogs and she allayed our concerns."

In September 2015, Noah boarded Greg Mahle's truck in Katy, Texas, to make the four-day journey to Andrea, Linda, and Sadie, his "forever" family. When Greg brought him out of the truck in Nanuet, New York, Andrea and Linda were waiting with a big sign that proclaimed "Gotcha Noah." Noah practically dragged Greg down the trailer steps, made a beeline to Andrea and Linda, tail wagging a mile a minute, and lavished them with kisses. There were others waiting to meet their dogs, too, but Noah somehow knew he was destined for Andrea and Linda.

"He has so much love to give," Linda told me. "Given the circumstances he was in, he wants nothing more than human contact. He wants to be in your lap, on your feet, or to lay his head on your chest and listen to your heart."

Sadie and Noah both go to work with Andrea, a freelance video editor, in Manhattan every day. Noah often sits at the video screens, looking intently at the images.

"He sometimes trounces Sadie," Linda told me, "but

as soon as it's over he wants to curl up with her. He loves her and Sadie feels close to him. We tried walking them separately one day but she was constantly looking for him."

As with Albie and us, the mystery of Noah's previous life is a subtle part of the bond between Noah and Linda and Andrea.

Why adopt a rescue dog? As Andrea says, "You have a purpose when you care for them. It gives your life meaning." Dogs who might have been dispatched from this world without a second thought within the cold concrete walls of a shelter now will know what it's like to have their heads stroked by someone who loves them.

"We don't know how he ended up on a trash pile in Melrose Park," said Linda, "but we think he had bonded with humans before because he was so caring and loving from the start. It's hard to imagine anyone would have given up on him."

"I try not to think about the days before he came to us," Andrea added. "I don't even see his scars anymore. He's such a happy dog that it's hard to think of him in that situation."

"Stephanie [Noah's foster] thinks he's forgotten all of it," said Linda. "Whatever he went through he's forgotten. We try to take our cues from him. He's so resilient. But we're very mindful of where he was."

Linda's job requires a lot of travel, so Andrea is Noah's primary caretaker.

"Noah loves being taken care of by Andrea," Linda added. "He relishes every little piece of attention she gives him. Unlike many dogs, he loves having his teeth brushed and his nails clipped."

"Noah has brought out the nurturer in me," said Andrea. "We don't have kids and I am probably the last woman on earth who would have a child. But I do all the baths and brushing and from the very beginning I referred to Noah as 'Noah baby!' I've never called another dog that."

Why adopt a rescue dog? As Andrea says, "You have a purpose when you care for them. It gives your life meaning."

Talking with Andrea and Linda, and later so many others who had welcomed a second-chance dog into their lives, I realized that we were all sharing a similar experience and similar feelings about that experience. The particulars might vary, but to a person we each felt a deep sense of fulfillment and satisfaction in being able to provide love, affection, and a warm place to sleep for a beautiful living creature that, as the famous line in "Amazing Grace" goes, had once been lost but now was found—a creature that was once abandoned or abused, or had never known a home or human kindness, or that might otherwise have been dispatched from this world without a second thought within the cold concrete walls of a shelter. Now these dogs were free to run through fields or jump into ponds or sit by fires and have their heads gently stroked by someone who loved them.

Jake celebrating life

CHAPTER TWO

Setting the World Right, One Dog at a Time

If you pick up a starving dog and make him prosperous
he will not bite you. This is the principal difference be-
tween a dog and man. —MARK TWAIN

IT DIDN'T TAKE LONG for us to have our first Albie crisis; three days after he first arrived in our home, to be exact. We'd left Albie home with our two sons, and Danny, home for the summer between his junior and senior years at Tulane University, inadvertently left the back door open. Within moments Albie was gone. Danny was beside himself with panic and when we arrived home about twenty minutes later he was out scouring the neighborhood and Noah was manning the home front. We were stunned. This sweet, precious dog we'd agreed to love and care for was missing. Just three days and we'd already failed him miserably.

Fortunately, the day Albie arrived in our home Danny insisted on using his own money to buy Albie an identification tag engraved with his name and our phone number. Within minutes of our arriving home, the phone rang. It was a woman who lived near the neighborhood elementary school, about a quarter mile away.

"I think we have your dog," she told Judy. "He's so sweet. My kids love him and want to keep him!"

Our relief was immeasurable, not least for Danny, who felt so responsible. The very next day we enclosed what had, until then, been only a partially fenced backyard. Clearly, after just three days, Albie had not yet come to identify us, and our home, as his own. That would come in due time, but meanwhile we couldn't help but start speculating about his past.

WHEN A DOG with a mysterious past comes into your home—and for the vast majority of rescue dogs their past *is* a mystery—it's natural to start making lots of assumptions. You observe a behavior and assume it's connected to something in that past. If the dog is skittish around men, for example, it's easy to assume the dog had some bad experience with a man, or men, in the past. If the dog fears sticks, it's easy to assume the dog was once beaten with one. But these assumptions may be way off the mark.

In those first few days, we were making all kinds of inferences about Albie's past. Judy and Noah surmised he'd never ridden in a car before. When they picked him up at the shelter he seemed to have no idea how to get into the car. And he wouldn't sit once inside, though that could just have been the excitement of being released from the shelter and into the hands of strangers. He seemed well mannered in the house, so we assumed he'd had a human family before.

But no amount of gentle coaxing at night would get him to climb the stairs and sleep in the bedroom. Instead, he slept underneath the coffee table in the living room and for the first few nights I slept on the sofa next to him. Maybe being under the table was like a little den to him; he seemed to feel safe there and, indeed, he still likes lying underneath tables and beds. We surmised that whatever house he'd lived in before, it didn't have stairs. But, really, we had no idea.

What was clear, however, was that the short, thirty-second video on which we'd based the momentous decision to adopt Albie did not lie. He was gentle and quiet (would the quiet part ever change!), and maybe we were projecting, but he seemed grateful, as if he somehow knew his worst days were behind him. He was also, thankfully, house-trained. He showed no interest in chasing a tennis ball (had anyone ever played fetch with him?), but he was so accommodating and easy that we, like Andrea and Linda with regard to their Noah, couldn't imagine anyone voluntarily letting him go. But then we came up with a theory.

> Rescue is all about setting the world right, one dog at a time.

In those very early days we took him to a couple of local spots where he could swim—nearby ponds where many local dogs cavort and play and splash around. It was July, after all, and what dog wouldn't welcome a watery respite from the heat? Whatever his genetic makeup, Albie clearly has a lot of Lab (he could be pure Lab, for all we know, despite the designation on his adoption papers as a Lab/golden retriever mix), and Labs, as everyone knows, love to swim. And they're called *retrievers* because they will swim into the water and retrieve waterfowl felled by a hunter. Well, Albie would not and, to this day, *will not* swim. He'll wade in up to his haunches, and he'll stand on the shore and bark at all the other dogs romping in the water like the goofy kid at camp who can't figure out how to fit in, but he will not swim.

So was born our theory that Albie had been someone's failed hunting dog, and in Louisiana a dog that won't hunt is lucky to live. While researching *Rescue Road* I learned that the end of hunting season in Louisiana coincides with a significant spike in stray dogs being brought to local shelters or picked up by animal control. And those are the lucky ones. So dispensable are dogs in some quarters that it's cheaper to dispatch a dog with a fifty-cent bullet and get a new dog for the next hunting season than feed him all winter, especially if he isn't adept at the purpose for which he was obtained. A hunter counting on Albie to swim out fifty yards to retrieve a duck would have been a very disappointed hunter. But truly, we don't know. There could be a wonderful family in Central Louisiana still wondering what became of their beloved yellow Lab.

There was one behavior, if you can call it that, that didn't exactly give us a window into Albie's previous life as much as it made our hearts break when we thought of him fending for himself in the wilds of Louisiana. Whether he'd been alone for weeks or months no one knows, but he'd been out there wandering. To this day, Albie trembles uncontrollably during thunderstorms no matter how tightly we hold him and how hard we try to reassure him. It's as if his central nervous system were wired right into the charged electrons swirling invisibly through the air. Now, many dogs react this way to thunderstorms, and fireworks, too. (We'll come to fireworks later.) But in those early days especially, as we'd try to reassure him through flashes of lightning and crashes of thunder, the thought of him caught outdoors in the middle of Louisiana with nowhere to turn and no one to comfort him saddened us deeply.

ONE OF OUR FIRST nearby water excursions with Albie was to the path that circles Lake Waban, half of which sits on property owned by Wellesley College. It's the path where we walked Reilly when he came to stay with us. I immediately got a taste of why people get such *na-chus* (that's Yiddish for satisfaction, pleasure, and contentment) from their dogs. Albie got plenty of compliments and admiration from passersby. We thanked them as if his adorability and sunny disposition somehow reflected on us, which, of course, they didn't. And with all the uncomplicated affection Albie was starting to show us, it was easy to feel virtuous and flatter ourselves, as if he had reserved all that love just for us because we were just so darned wonderful. But the truth is Albie could have been plunked down in any one of a million homes and he'd have been just as trusting, sweet, and loving. So we felt very lucky that he had fallen in with us. But, at the risk of sounding self-serving, he was really lucky to be with us, too.

OVER THE PAST FEW YEARS I've met and spoken with countless people who have given a lucky dog a second chance at life. But one story in particular drove home just how fortunate some dogs have to be to know love and kindness in this life, and the emotional sacrifice it can involve by those who make it possible.

In 2011, Brad and Staicey Scholtz of Vermilion, Ohio, adopted Jake, an eleven-and-a-half-year-old purebred yellow Lab. Jake had lived the first ten years of his life chained in a small yard behind a trailer home. In rain and snow and summer heat he was outside, caked in mud. His owner once burned Jake's skin trying to treat fleas with a pesticide. Jake never knew the joy of a simple walk, let alone a run through the woods or a swim in a cool pond. A neighbor who had watched Jake suffer year after year finally persuaded his owner to surrender him to the rescue organization she ran.

Coincidentally, Jake later found sanctuary at a large farm in Medina, Ohio, owned by Sarah Steiner, a Lab breeder from whom Brad and Staicey had acquired their first Lab in 1994. Brad and Staicey had been looking to adopt an older dog because they raise puppies for Canine Companions for Independence (CCI), a California-based organization that trains service dogs for people with disabilities. They raise each puppy to eighteen months, at which point it is evaluated. If it doesn't have the potential to be a service dog another permanent home is sought, and Brad and Staicey always wanted to be prepared to keep a puppy that didn't meet the strict criteria required to be a service dog. Having an older dog, they felt, would give them that flexibility. For many people, having two young dogs can be a real handful, and often an older dog helps train the younger one in the ways of the world.

When they came across Jake's picture and profile posted online, they contacted Sarah Steiner and decided to have a look. Sarah never expected Jake to find a forever home—he was too old and untrained—but the Scholtzes decided to meet Jake anyway.

"Jake came out and gave us a quick sniff," Staicey told me, "but you could tell he'd been alone all his life. He had no socialization, no training, and he'd never lived in a house, but he was beautiful and we took him on a trial basis. He was wild and crazy and very anxious. He bowled over everything. He was a freight train with fur.

"But there was something about him," added Staicey.

"I think we can do this!" Brad told her, and they made the commitment.

It wasn't easy. Jake had to be treated for heartworm (simple and inexpensive to prevent, but difficult and costly to treat). One day he scarfed down six chicken breasts and a bratwurst Brad had left unattended briefly, and within the first two weeks ran away and was found nearly forty miles away in Cleveland. But Brad and Staicey came to believe Jake was "sent to us from above."

Despite all he had been through, and all he had suffered at human hands, Jake was a lover. "Brad said Jake taught him how to love," Staicey told me. "That you have to appreciate and be grateful for every day and have no bitterness. Every day is a new day." It's a sentiment I would hear many, many times when I asked people what they'd learned from adopting a rescue dog.

Just eight months later Brad and Staicey faced a terrible decision. Jake was diagnosed with osteosarcoma, an aggressive cancer. He was not yet in pain, but the vet told them he soon would be. Because he had suffered for so many years, Brad and Staicey were determined not to let him suffer another day. But it never seemed the right day to help Jake cross what dog lovers call the Rainbow

Bridge. One Monday they felt the time had come, and in a field, with Brad and Staicey by his side, their veterinarian helped ease Jake over the bridge.

"He left this world knowing someone loved him and that he had a home where he was wanted," Staicey told me. They drew comfort from a friend who told them, "You taught Jake what heaven would be like."

Finding adoptive homes for older dogs is very challenging; few people are willing to make the emotional investment in a dog they know will be with them for just a short time. But, as Jake's story demonstrates, the quality of the experience is not related to the quantity— what Jake and the Scholtzes gave each other in just a short time is immeasurable.

IF THERE'S AN ACTUAL HEAVEN on earth for lucky dogs, it just might be a forty-five-acre farm in southern Vermont where Adrienne Finney, an occupational therapist, lives with a brood of yellow and black and chocolate rescued Labs that, in the summer of 2016, numbered ten. Adrienne is well known among Lab lovers in the Northeast. She documents virtually every day on the farm with spectacular photographs she posts to Facebook. Her Facebook followers really get to know the dogs by name and personality and follow their trials, triumphs, and antics closely. Adrienne is an astute observer and records the progress of each addition to the group as they acclimate to life on the farm with the other dogs, the various relationships that form between and among them, and the three horses and five cats that also call the farm home.

Adrienne's Labs have known all kinds of deprivation. Percy was confined to a room with a severely autistic teenager who beat him mercilessly. When Percy finally snapped back one day the mother threw him out of a car along Interstate 95. Henry came from a shelter in New York City after being confiscated from an abusive owner. Molly was crated twenty-two hours a day with no companionship until she was nine months old and the family offered her up on Craigslist. The family he'd lived with all his life surrendered Sam to a rescue organization. He was suffering from frostbite (he was left outside in good weather and bad), severe arthritis, and parasites. Oscar was a local dog, from Guilford, Vermont, where he'd lived on a chain for all eight of his years.

It can take remarkable patience and persistence to socialize and alleviate the anxiety and other behavioral issues such damaged dogs can (but don't always) exhibit. Most are resilient enough to bounce back quickly; others require more time.

The Guilford Gang, as Adrienne's brood is known, started with the late Homer in 2009, a shelter dog from Tennessee and Adrienne's first rescue, though she had other dogs living with her at the time.

"Homer started the gathering of the Labs," Adrienne

told me. "It grew after the other dogs died and it was just Homer and me. I felt Homer needed a playmate. That's when I got Henry out of a terrible holding facility in New York City. He was terrified at first, but he really wanted Homer to play—he'd nip Homer's legs to try and engage him—but Homer just wanted companionship."

So Adrienne started looking for a more active play-mate for Henry, which led her to George, picked up as a stray at just four months after being abused in a program that matches puppies with prisoners. There are many excellent puppies-and-prisoners programs around the country, programs in which prisoners socialize rescued pups and ready them for adoption while giving the pris-oners a meaningful experience that helps many of them learn compassion. (We'll meet one ex-convict later who left prison with the rescue dog he trained.) The program George came from was eventually shut down. George spent the next seven months in a boarding facility while Labs4rescue (the organization Albie came from) looked for a home. Then Adrienne's home became his.

Henry and George became fast friends. But when they started ganging up on Winnie, another yellow Lab Adrienne had adopted from the same New York facility where she found Henry, Adrienne went looking for a girlfriend for Winnie and adopted Lila from a New Hampshire rescue.

And so the Guilford Gang grew and grew; the most recent arrivals, as of the summer of 2016, were Peter and

Martin, a pair of senior Labs, twelve and eight years old, respectively.

Despite the numbers, there is nothing remotely similar about life on the farm for the Guilford Gang and a hoarding situation, of which there are, tragically, far too many.

"Every one of my dogs gets a lot of individual attention," Adrienne told me, and it's clear from her keen observations about each, and my own visit, that that's the case. "They live in my house, not in crates, and sleep in the bedroom. My house is clean and well appointed. All the dogs are well trained and spend a lot of time outdoors. They live the same life as if I had just two. When you rescue a dog it's a promise to give them a high quality of life, to help them thrive, not just exist."

Winnie is an excellent example of the individualized attention and patience it can take to help each of the dogs who come to the farm live a full life. Winnie had spent months in a small cage in a New York City shelter. When she first came to the farm she couldn't walk a straight line. She kept spinning in a circle.

"I thought the best thing I could do was take her to the beach," Adrienne told me. "But she was too freaked out by the open space. At home that first week she kept retreating to her crate and I slept with her in the crate on the bathroom floor. She couldn't even handle the open space of a room. It took a week before she started walking forward."

And Winnie was so fearful of the other dogs, Adrienne had to introduce them one at a time. "I had a friend hold Homer when I introduced Winnie to him and Winnie tried to take his face off. After ten seconds she stopped and realized Homer wasn't going to hurt her and they were good after that. I repeated the process with each of the dogs." Today peace reigns over the farm where the members of the Guilford Gang enjoy lives any dog would envy, thanks to one woman with a very big heart.

As Adrienne's experience shows, every rescue dog comes with its own set of challenges, for each has lived a unique life. Though the majority adapt quickly and easily, some will require patience and fortitude. But the reward is in watching the dogs come into their own and seeing their fears melt away as they take their place in their new family, whether they are an only dog or one of a pack like the Guilford Gang. For homeless dogs such Albie and Noah and Jake and Homer and Winnie, "rescue" is all about setting the world right, one dog at a time.

It can take remarkable patience and persistence to socialize and alleviate the anxiety and other behavioral issues damaged dogs can (but don't always) exhibit. Most are resilient enough to bounce back quickly; others require more time.

Rosco enjoying a swim

CHAPTER THREE

Home Is Where
the Dog Is

*The love of a dog is a pure thing. He gives you a trust
which is total. You must not betray it.*
—MICHEL HOUELLEBECQ

WHEN A DOG is willing to sit for hours and stare
out the window waiting for you to come home,
it's safe to say he is now bonded to you as if with Super
Glue. And there's no denying how flattering that can be.
Albie's growing attachment to us, which manifested in
part in his desire for physical contact, brought me right
back to the days when my boys, then toddlers, would fall
asleep on my shoulder or chest and everything seemed
right with the world.

Though his affection for us was growing, in those
early weeks Albie continued to sleep under the coffee
table in the living room and refused to come upstairs.
Until he was comfortable everywhere in our home, until
he was no longer fearful of what might lie at the other
end of the stairs, I didn't think he would truly be *home*,

for *home* implies that place where we feel safest and most secure. Home isn't just where we keep our things, eat our meals, and hang our hat. Home is, or should be, a place where we *belong*, where we are loved unconditionally, and where we are comforted. Is there a word in the English language more evocative, and more comforting, than *home*?

I wasn't sure how we would know when Albie finally felt he had found his home, whether he would send us a signal, whether there would be a eureka moment, or whether it would be a process so gradual we might never even notice until after the fact. All I could do was watch and wait.

Elissa Altman is a writer famous for her James Beard Award–winning food blog *Poor Man's Feast* (and a book of the same name). She also writes a recurring *Washington Post* column, "Feeding My Mother." She and her partner of nearly two decades, Susan, live in Newtown, Connecticut. (Yes, *that* Newtown, where the Sandy Hook Elementary School massacre occurred in 2012. More on that later.)

In 2009, Elissa and Susan adopted a seven-year-old yellow Lab mix named Addie. She'd been used to produce multiple litters of puppies, likely for sale, in a backyard in Arkansas, and when she stopped breeding she was dumped by her human family at a high-kill shelter. Though she had a liver condition and was overweight, Elissa and Susan, who found her online, were smitten and gave her a home. (Sadly, Addie died just a few weeks before Elissa and I spoke in midsummer of 2016.)

"When we adopted Addie I wasn't working at home full-time, so we took ten days off to get her used to our house and the neighbors and their dogs," Elissa told me. "On the third day we decided to go out and leave her alone for just a short time, about fifteen minutes, to see how she would do. She was a little panicky when we left, but we didn't feel like she needed to be in a crate. We weren't worried about that."

When they came back, there on Addie's bed in the living room were a pair of sunglasses, a sweater, a garden boot, and the television remote. Addie had spent her time alone gathering items of Elissa's and Susan's and placing them, unharmed, on her bed.

Another day, Elissa said, "We came home and there she was on her bed with a bottle of wine and the phone." Addie had pulled the bottle from an open case on the floor. To Elissa and Susan this was their sign that Addie was *home*.

But for others the process is gradual and prolonged and there is no single moment that signals, *I'm home*.

Allison Smith and her husband, Tom McManus, of Athens, New York, have adopted nine dogs since 1987 through various rescue organizations in New York, Colorado, and Connecticut, some pulled from southern shelters. Many have, or had, Sesotho names. Sesotho is the language spoken in Lesotho, Africa, where Allison served as a Peace Corps volunteer in the 1980s.

Kekeletso ("Keke" for short) came from a collie rescue in upstate New York. She'd been picked up as a stray in Oneonta, New York, after being sighted several times over the course of a month.

"She was so frightened," Allison told me. "But her background was a puzzle. We never knew whether or why she was dumped on the street." Of all their dogs, Keke was the toughest when it came to helping her feel she'd come home.

"It took a lot of time and patience," said Allison. The other dog in their household at the time was Dino, a female yellow Lab. Only Dino's company seemed to help Keke feel safe. "We had to bring Dino with us wherever we went or Keke wouldn't get in the car. She couldn't tell us her story, so we had to go with what she was telling us," and she was telling them she wanted to be with Dino. "It was all very gradual," said Allison. "I can't pinpoint a moment when she felt she was home."

Whether it's a specific moment or a gradual process, a dog's "homecoming" is one of the great joys of rescuing a second-chance dog. It's the moment when the dog is no longer a stranger in your midst, but a member of the family.

———

RONNIE STANLEY, on the other hand, can identify the exact moment his recue dog Lola announced she was home. A few weeks before, in the summer of 2016, Ronnie had walked into a Baltimore shelter with his girlfriend, Emily, and a teammate. He never expected his adoption of Lola would become a national news story, but when you're a first-round NFL draft pick of the Baltimore Ravens about to start your rookie season, and you're six feet six inches tall and weigh about 350 pounds, you tend to get noticed.

When the shelter staff learned who he was, they recognized an opportunity to encourage others to follow Ronnie's example. The story quickly gained traction and made Ronnie Stanley a local hero to animal lovers and advocates.

"I wanted a hard-to-adopt dog," Ronnie told me by phone from his boyhood home in Las Vegas before leaving for the Ravens training camp in the summer of 2016. "One that wouldn't be helped. It was something I knew I could do."

Lola is a pit bull mix that had been overbred. (Because of their undeserved reputation as dangerous dogs, pit bulls are especially hard to adopt out.) Her tummy and her teats sag and won't be returning to normal. But Ronnie looked right past that.

Lola let Ronnie know she was home when Ronnie

took a leap of faith by leaving Lola alone. "One day I had to leave and left her alone in my room with all my stuff, hoping nothing would happen." Ronnie came home and everything was exactly where he'd left it. "She didn't disrupt anything. She knew this was her place." Lola was home.

Whether it's a specific moment or a gradual process, a dog's "homecoming" is one of the great joys of rescuing a second-chance dog. You finally feel you can count on and trust them—to be faithful, to not run away, to be responsive to you in ways they are not with others. And they know they can count on you—to comfort them when they are scared, to feed them when they are hungry, to rub their bellies when they want affection. It's the moment when the dog is no longer a stranger in your midst, but a member of the family.

SOMETIMES A DOG will even insist on showing the people around her where she considers home. Heather Fuqua lives in Pineville, Louisiana, which is something of a ground zero for dogs desperately in need of homes. Pineville is across the Red River from Alexandria, where Albie spent five months in the shelter. There are many thousands of stray and abandoned dogs in the area. Heather has been fostering dogs for Keri Toth, Albie's adoption coordinator, for many years.

Heather's dachshund, Sweetheart, was abandoned,

pregnant, in the midsummer Louisiana heat at a baseball field, left in her crate with a bag of dog food on
top. A Good Samaritan took her home until she gave
birth to her pups, which the Good Samaritan adopted
out, and she then brought Sweetheart to her veterinarian's office and declared she didn't want to keep her
any longer.

The vet called Keri, known throughout the area as a
dog savior, and Keri called Heather to see if she could
foster. Heather took her in.

"Whoever owned her took good care of her," Heather
told me. "She was heartworm-negative [suggesting she
was regularly given a heartworm preventive]. No one
knows why she was dumped. I had her spayed and she
was adopted by a woman in Pineville. But she quickly
ran away. After she'd been missing for a couple of days
the adopter called and I went out with my sister-in-law,
my sister-in-law's mom, and my daughter, Addyson, who
was two and a half, to try and find her. We found her
near her new home but she wouldn't come to us. Addyson was sitting in the field nearby and she called her
and the dog came over and sat right in her lap.

"I was determined not to keep her," added Heather.
"We had three dogs already. So I found another home
but she ran away again, right through the front door.
Again we scoured the neighborhood, but again only Addyson could get her to come. We realized she was saying
that her home was with us. Addyson used to put her in

a baby stroller and walk her around the house and they became best friends."

SOMETIMES THE PRESENCE of another dog helps a new arrival feel at home right away. Kelly and Gregory Thompson of Brandford, Connecticut, had a black Lab named Maci when they adopted a second rescue dog, Estelle, a senior, in 2013. "Seniors" such as Estelle and the Scholtz family's Jake are dogs roughly six years old or older, and can be harder for rescue organizations to place, either because people are reluctant to have their time with a dog shortened or because dogs, like humans, are likely to encounter more health challenges as they age.

"We expected it would take some time for Maci and Estelle to get to know one another," said Kelly, "but within twenty minutes they were nose to nose on the dog bed. It was a very easy transition." Estelle moved in and made the Thompsons' home her own straightaway.

Dogs that have been in a foster home may also have an easier time making the transition into their adopting families; fearful or distrusting dogs may overcome their fears while in foster care and feel at home more quickly when they are placed. Since adopting Rosco, a yellow Lab, in 2009, Nancy Allen-Ziemski of Norwich, Connecticut, has fostered nearly three dozen dogs on their road to adoption. Some are with her for only a matter of days before they move on to their forever homes; some stay for weeks. One, Bella, was a "foster failure," meaning Nancy decided to make her home Bella's forever home.

"I feel like I'm pet-sitting for people I don't know yet," Nancy told me. But whether the dogs are with her for days, weeks, or months, the experience can accelerate the process of feeling at home once a forever family is found.

"I've seen dogs that come in terrified of the world and you can see them change quickly," Nancy told me. "They are so resilient. They may have been hurt or neglected but they're ready to trust humans again. Every single one has overcome, though it takes some longer than others. They all leave more secure and more comfortable than when they came."

Rosco helps the process. "He's my big mentor," added Nancy. "He's a bundle of happy energy, a big friendly goof. But he's calm and gentle with the fosters and he teaches them. So many of the dogs have no idea how to play when they arrive. It's so sad. Occasionally a foster gets in his face and he growls, but he's a teacher."

Music is part of the foster experience for the dogs when they stay with Nancy.

"I play violin for the dogs. Rosco sings with me, howls along, really," Nancy added. "The fosters are so curious about the violin. Some are a little afraid. Some lie down and listen and just hang out while I play." Helping dogs prepare for their forever homes, "giving them a second chance at the life they deserve, makes me feel more complete," Nancy told me. And she makes the dogs feel more at ease living in a home.

NOT ALL DOGS, or, to be more precise, not all adopters, have the benefit of a foster parent or family to help prepare their dog for life in a new home. Nor do they come into homes with another dog to comfort them, as Maci comforted Estelle, or teach them, as Rosco has so many others.

Albie didn't have the benefit of foster care, or even of a doggie companion, when he came to us in 2012. He came directly from the noisy and austere environment of a high-kill shelter. Getting him to feel at home—indeed, teaching him to live in a home, one where he would sometimes have to be alone—was uncharted territory for him and for us. Like Elissa Altman and her partner Susan's experience, those first experiments with leaving Albie alone were fraught with uncertainty.

On our first "date" after Albie came to live with us, Judy and I went to the movies to see *Beasts of the Southern Wild*. Appropriately enough, it's set in Louisiana, where Albie was found as a stray, and Albie was himself something of a beast of the southern wild.

The boys were both out, so this was Albie's first time home by himself. It felt exactly the same as it had years earlier when we first left the kids in the hands of babysitters. They'd cry and reach out for us, and we'd watch, cringing, from the car and see their tear-streaked faces in the window as a game babysitter tried to cheer them up and they waved good-bye to Mommy and Daddy. It was like having a piece of your heart ripped out every time. It never got easier, but we needed some alone time . . . together.

At least with a babysitter you can call home and make sure everyone is still alive. Albie was alone and we hadn't taught him to answer the phone, so we came directly home after the movie. No coffee or late-night bite to eat. As I climbed the front steps, I looked into the window that framed the front entrance of the house where we lived at the time, and there was Albie, lying down as close to the door as he possibly could. He had almost surely been in that same spot for two hours, just waiting and wondering if and when we'd be coming back.

It took him a good ten minutes to settle down after we walked in. I patted his belly; he put his paws on my arms to keep me near. I rubbed his head; his tail thumped the floor in joy. I nuzzled his neck; he threw his front leg over my shoulder.

That night I had a vivid and powerful dream—one from which I awoke in real terror—that his previous owner, or "his human," as some like to say (if indeed he ever had one), had located him and was trying to get him back. I woke up feeling that I would fight like hell for this dog, that we belonged together and it would be till death do us part. We were definitely bonding, but was he *home?*

At this point Albie had been with us for about a month, still sleeping under the coffee table in the living room. Then, one evening, I couldn't find him. I knew he was in the house and our downstairs comprised only five rooms—easy to check in half a minute. I called him, but no response. Could he be upstairs at last? I climbed the stairs and made the right turn into our bedroom. And there, curled up on our bed, was Albie.

I'll never forget the plaintive look in his dark brown eyes and the uncertain expression on his face. He seemed to be asking, *Is this okay?*

I had come a long way just agreeing to have a dog, but I had vowed, "No dog in the bed." One look in his eyes and I knew he was not only *home* but, if he so chose, in the bed to stay. We had earned his trust and his love. That dream I'd had a few nights before was my signal to myself that he was home. But it was by his literal and figurative leap of faith into our bed that he told us he, too, knew he was home.

Different dogs may express this in different ways, and for some it may not come in one crystallized moment, but be alert for it, because no moment with your rescue dog will be more precious or more satisfying than the one when he or she tells you, *I'm home.* Whether you realized it or not when you decided to adopt a rescue dog, this was your purpose all along.

———

THE CHALLENGE OF leaving Albie home alone occasion-ally without feeling guilty, fearing that he might think we were abandoning him, was formidable. And there's nothing quite as guilt-inducing as a dog who tilts his head slightly and glares at you with baleful eyes as you close the door behind you.

But leaving Albie alone for short periods was just a practice run, of sorts, for the inevitable times in the fu-ture when we would have to leave him for longer periods in the care of others. Though we take Albie and our second rescue dog, Salina (whom we'll meet formally a little later), as often as we can when we travel by car, there are trips where bringing them just isn't practical, and, frankly, just as when our kids were young, some-times you just need a few days, not just a quick trip to the movies, with your spouse or partner or just by your-self. Most of us do, anyway.

After he'd been with us about eight months, Judy and I took our first trip without Albie. And did we ever feel guilty! I wished desperately I could explain the con-cept of a temporary absence to him. But I was also aware there would be something neurotic and overboard about refusing to travel without him, even as I fretted I would be scarring him for life. To this day, Albie gets a little depressed when he sees me packing a suitcase. He knows what it means, though he doesn't seem to have as much separation anxiety as I do. (Often anxious dogs will, when left alone, become destructive, and he's never been destructive.)

> Leaving your dog at home by itself for the first time after you adopt is like leaving your kids home with a babysitter for the first time—heartwrenching and utterly guilt-inducing. If only we could explain that we *will* be back!

On our very first trip without Albie we were gone four nights in Key West. Albie stayed home with our son Noah, then seventeen, and Katie, the then-twenty-five-year-old daughter of friends. Left to his own devices, Noah, a high school senior at the time, would likely have forgotten to go to school, eat, sleep, and otherwise do the minimum necessary for human survival. About the third day it might have occurred to him that Albie hadn't eaten or been outside in a while. Hence Katie. Here was one of my concerns about getting a dog, fully realized—that it would seriously cramp our freedom just as we were reaching the stage in life when we wouldn't be tied down with kids.

Just a year earlier the idea of having a dog was about as appealing as owning an iguana (with apologies to lizard lovers), and now I was turning to Jell-O at the thought of leaving Albie for a few days. It didn't help when we learned Albie was pining for us, too: he spent the first twenty-four hours on the window seat watching for our return. And when we did come home he went bonkers, which made me feel both terrible (he missed us!) and great (he loves us!). It gets you to wondering what dogs make of our absences; how, if at all, they measure the time when we're away, and if the feeling of "missing" another is experienced as we experience it. So much of a relationship with a dog is deducing what's going on in that head of theirs, or projecting our feelings onto their emotional palettes. But where I was once dubious about a dog's ability to love, I'm now a believer.*

As for travel? The passage of time hasn't made it any easier. We might look forward to being free of the demands of caring for two dogs now (well, actually three, but we'll come to that later), but we miss them when we're away and worry for them. No trip without the dogs is planned without guilt and a tinge of sadness. It probably says more about me than about dogs, but leaving a dog that has known some form of deprivation is far tougher than I ever imagined it would be. Once they become part of your life, home is where the dog is, and, to coin a phrase, there's no place like home, especially when there's a dog waiting for you by the door.

---

*This isn't to say, however, it's just like the love *between two human beings*, just that dogs are capable of what we would describe as love.

Zosia finds a new friend

CHAPTER FOUR

Life Isn't Always a Beach . . . but Sometimes It Is

I'm suspicious of people who don't like dogs, but I trust a dog when it doesn't like a person. —BILL MURRAY

AFTER A FEW WEEKS IN OUR HOME, Albie had made the entire house his own, except the basement; he would never venture into the subterranean depths. In so doing he had completed the long journey he'd been on, one that began in rural Louisiana in circumstances unknown to us. This sweet and earnest dog, once lost, and now found, had made his way to us thanks to a series of lucky breaks that elude so many others. While he was wandering alone he was sleeping outdoors or in whatever shelter he could find, and, after he'd been picked up by animal control in Rapides Parish, Louisiana, had spent five months sleeping on the concrete floor of a high-kill shelter. Now he was sleeping on a mattress with sheets and blankets and a family that adored him.

With each passing day, Albie became more and more

"ours," and we "his," but we watched his interactions with other dogs and other people very carefully; we were, after all, on a steep learning curve about Albie in particular and dogs in general. We all want our dogs to be perfect—to interact with others, canine and human, predictably and nicely. But dogs, like people, don't like everyone they meet and their behavior toward others can evolve over time.

As mild-mannered as he was, Albie still needed some basic training. When he came to us he didn't know even the most basic of all commands, "Sit!" So we enrolled in a training class for beginners (that term applying to both the dogs and their people). There's no reason a dog needs to learn to roll over on command, or to shake hands, as cute as that is, or to balance a treat on the end of its nose. But some basic training is needed to ensure a dog stays safe ("come"), doesn't bother unsuspecting strangers ("stay"), or generally understands that some manners are required to live in harmony in a home populated by people ("sit").

When we went to the first class I had all the same feelings I had when our kids started school: I wanted Albie to do well, to behave well, and, frankly, to not embarrass us, as that was something we were perfectly capable of doing all by ourselves. We wanted Albie to be a good student. We wanted him to succeed.

When he learned quickly, we felt like proud parents. When he peed on the classroom floor two minutes into the first class, we were mortified. He proved overall to be adept at learning basic commands, and was mostly gentle and sociable in class and at home. However, there was one type of person that made him uneasy and whose presence immediately provoked growling and fear in Albie: adolescent males, especially our younger son Noah's friends. Given how friendly he was in general, we were perturbed by this strange behavior around teenage boys. It was our first realization that living with a dog wasn't going to be one continuous Hallmark moment.

It would be easy to assume that he'd had a bad experience or suffered at the hands of one or more teenage boys in his past. But that's not necessarily so. Our other rescue dog, Salina, came to us as a young puppy, and has always displayed a fear of small children. While writing my previous book, *Rescue Road*, I had the good fortune to meet the family in rural Louisiana whose dog had given birth to her. Yet, despite never having been around small children (and thus having no reason to be afraid of them), whenever she sees one, her body stiffens, the hair on her back stands up, and she starts, not growling exactly, but harrumphing.

One day, while walking Salina and Albie at Elm Bank, the preserve along the Charles River where I walked almost daily with Albie when he first arrived, we encountered a father with several small children. Salina launched into her usual routine.

"I'm sorry," I said. "She's afraid of children."

"That's okay," replied the father. "So am I."

Clearly, Albie and Salina each have innate fears or fearful instincts that we'll never be able to understand or help them overcome, as we thought we would. We struggled—and continue years later to struggle—with this behavior and to make sense of the infinite amount of contradictory advice on how to manage it. Much as I hate to admit it, we haven't succeeded in changing it. If anything, in Albie's case, it's gotten worse with time.

ONE OF THE STRESSORS of having a dog with such fears is that many people don't understand. They'll allow their children to run up to a dog on a leash, arms outstretched, expecting that picture-perfect interaction, and are surprised and sometimes even annoyed or angry when the dog doesn't respond as they expect. Often, the not-so-subtle implication is that you haven't properly trained or raised the dog.

Dogs, like people, have their fears and anxieties. You wouldn't expect a child to necessarily be happy to have a big, enthusiastic dog run toward *them* and start licking *their* face. Similarly, you can't expect a dog to necessarily be happy to have a child, or group of children, run toward them screaming and start putting their hands on the dog's face and pulling its tail.

Nevertheless, Albie's reaction to Noah's friends was distressing. It was our home, too, after all, and we wanted all of our guests to feel safe and welcome. Their arrival at our house, a non-event before Albie, was now always fraught with tension. Every time they arrived, or came downstairs to raid the fridge or to leave, we had to be alert. We'd hold Albie by the collar and try and distract him with a treat or comfort him. He never nipped or bit anyone, but if we hadn't been vigilant, who knows? And no matter what we tried—having the boys give him the treats, for example—he never overcame the fear. In fact, he even started to exhibit the same behavior around friends of ours he knew well and had even been affectionate with. They'd get up from the dinner table and he'd trot up behind them and bark and use his muzzle to nudge them. We've worked with trainers and tried various techniques to try to reverse the trend, to little avail.

Over time he has also become more unpredictable with other dogs. In the early days, the first two years or so, he would run off-leash at Elm Bank and I never worried about his interactions with other dogs. He'd bark with excitement sometimes, enjoyed games of chase and even some roughhousing, but never displayed aggression. That, too, changed.

During our second year with Albie, a new kid (a canine kid) arrived on the block—a Vizsla named Crosby. Vizslas are a lean, houndlike breed of Hungarian origin known for their high energy and speed. For whatever reason, Crosby and Albie, each perfectly sweet on his own, took an instant dislike to each other.

Albie had reached the point where we were comfortable with him off-leash in the front yard (except, of course, when Noah's friends were expected to arrive). He rarely wandered far, though he sometimes chased squirrels through the neighbors' yards. And he often went to visit our across-the-street neighbors, Seth and Linda, and their Bernese mountain dog, the ever-gentle Ivy. (Our tiny private way had virtually no car traffic.)

Crosby often wandered around off-leash. From their first meeting he and Albie were at loggerheads, and we had to be cautious about letting him off-leash thereafter. Each encounter was tense, to say the least, and, left untended, seemed poised to turn violent. Even when we took on-leash walks down the street, Crosby would appear and it was like trying to keep two enraged hockey players apart. We had to adjust. The picture I had of a perfectly behaved and gentle dog was proving unrealistically optimistic. What confounded me was that in most circumstances he was as sweet and gentle as could be. There just seemed to be these triggers.

Gradually, Albie's reaction to other male dogs, not just Crosby, became more and more problematic. Sometimes encounters with other males went perfectly fine, but others involved growling, ears back, fur on the back raised—all signs of aggression or fear. I often found myself explaining from a distance that he sometimes didn't do well with other male dogs. But invariably other dogs, off-leash, would come bounding right up to us only to have Albie growl and bark ominously. I found myself apologizing a lot; my entreaties that he was really a sweet dog probably sounded utterly unpersuasive. There didn't seem to be any pattern to the dogs Albie liked and disliked, with one exception. He didn't like Vizslas, even if they weren't Crosby. Every time he saw a Vizsla, male or female, the reaction was the same. I was astonished that he seemed able to recognize other dogs by breed, at least dogs of this particular breed.

Increasingly we had to keep him on his leash wherever we went, even as Salina ran free during our walks in the woods. I felt so badly for him. He was being deprived of what he loved most—running free through the trees and over the logs—and I couldn't explain to him that he was, unfortunately, bringing it on himself.

When the trails seemed empty I would occasionally let him off his leash, but as soon as I saw a dog in the distance I'd call him back and leash him. Then, one day, we rounded a bend and before I knew it Albie was on top of a shy and harmless Vizsla walking with a man and a woman. It was the first and only time I've seen him actually attack another dog. The man quickly lifted Albie and tossed him aside, and before I could utter a word of apology he was berating me. He was angry, and justifiably so. But I wasn't the irresponsible dog "owner" he accused me of being; I was aware and trying my best to head off volatile situations while trying to let Albie do what dogs love to do. In this one instance everything happened so quickly I was unable to prevent it.

My hopes that Albie would get beyond whatever was leading to his increased anxiety, especially around other male dogs, were dashed. Since the change in behavior roughly coincided with Salina's arrival, we thought perhaps he was being protective of her, but we don't really know.

We now have strategies for managing these encounters, but Albie is no longer allowed the freedom he once had. Now, when we walk in the woods, and almost always on the beach, Albie is leashed. This was especially sad when we returned to South Carolina for an extended midwinter stay for the third time in early 2016.

Much as we'd like it to be, living with a dog (rescue or not) isn't going to be one continuous Hallmark moment.

Albie loves the snow, but we hate it, so we had started escaping. On our first two trips Albie was free to run on the beach, and *did he ever run*. He has never seemed as free as he did running on that beach. Every morning and afternoon a gaggle of people and dogs gather on the beach in front of where we stay and the dogs have a ball. It's a big, happy play group. But when we returned in early 2016, we couldn't let Albie join the gang as he had previously. He just got too amped up and we didn't think we could trust him.

Judy would take Salina to play with the group while I walked Albie, on-leash, elsewhere.

There were times when our kids were little and suffered from some slight or temporary ostracism from their peers and we would try to cheer them up by having some special "mommy-and-daddy" time. We'd try to distract them from their hurt by pretending it was just as much fun watching a movie with us or going out for ice cream, but we knew better and, frankly, so did they. That's precisely how I felt when Albie and I walked alone while all the other dogs were having a field day at the beach. I don't know if he missed being at the beach with the group—whether as we walked he had an image of all these other dogs frolicking together—but I certainly did, and I wished he could have been part of it.

But there were also moments when I felt elated for Albie at the beach. Since we are in South Carolina during the off-season, we often have long stretches of beach to ourselves. When we do, we still let Albie off-leash and take great pleasure in watching him and Salina exult in their freedom.

One day we saw a dolphin making its way along the beach about twenty yards from shore. Albie spotted it, too, and he took off running to keep up. Salina followed. He couldn't hear us calling him over the sounds of the waves, but he was likely too far into his obsession with the chase to respond even if he could hear us. Soon he and Salina were a few hundred yards ahead of us on a stretch of sandbar separated from the beach by about twenty feet of water. When Salina broke toward the beach to run back to us she plunged into the water and we saw immediately that it was quite deep. But we knew she could swim. At the lake in the Berkshires, in western Massachusetts, near the cottage we used to own she was always swimming after tossed sticks as Albie watched goofily from the shore and barked at her. As Albie followed Salina in hot pursuit across the sandbar, everything seemed to suddenly go into slow motion. Albie, for the first time in our life with him, was unwittingly about to plunge into water over his head. I saw him go under and was prepared to go in after him. We were still a good distance away and I started to run. It probably took all of three seconds but it seemed an eternity until his head emerged and he swam to shore. We'd never seen him swim before and haven't since, but I felt like a proud daddy when he did. "I knew you could do it!"

We always suspected that if he had to he could swim—all dogs can, we thought—but still we felt overjoyed for him, a joy way out of proportion to the occasion. So much of what we feel around dogs seems irrational and out of proportion, and that's one of the things I love about having dogs. I never imagined when we decided to adopt a dog how intensely I would project my own feelings onto their emotional lives. I doubt, for example, that Albie experienced our walks while Salina was romping with the other dogs on the beach the way either of the kids would have experienced it, as an outcast—I surely felt worse than he did about it—nor did I realize how proud and happy I'd feel when they succeeded.

But all of this made me realize that dogs, like children, have their challenges and some children, and some dogs, are easier than others. Life isn't a beach all the time for any of us, so we have to savor and celebrate the moments when it is and push through the tough times when it's not. And just as we don't surrender our children when things veer off course or become challenging, the commitment to a dog, especially one that had to beat long odds just to make it home, ought to run just as deep. There are times when circumstances may make it necessary to rehome or surrender a dog, but it should never be a matter of convenience. A dog that has known deprivation, hunger, abuse, neglect, or the loneliness of a high-kill shelter deserves every chance to succeed. Unless they are a danger, or you are incapable of providing properly for them for some reason, you just don't give up on them. Ever.

CONSIDER, FOR EXAMPLE, Amy and Ken Lovett of Troy, New York, who adopted a Lab mix, Guinness (fifteen years old when we spoke in the summer of 2016), when she was just a three-month-old puppy.

"She didn't know how to be a puppy and we didn't

know how to care for a puppy," Amy told me. When Guinness was three they felt she needed a companion. "When we visited friends with a dog she acted like a dog. She just seemed so much better when she was around other dogs."

So the Lovetts went on PetFinder, a Web site many rescue organizations use to post profiles of their adoptable pets, and found Bo, an adult of indeterminate breed that Amy described as looking like a dog put together by committee. They arranged with Bo's foster for Guinness and Bo to meet before making the commitment. The two dogs were smitten and Bo also took to Amy right away. But Bo lived only a year and a half before lymphoma forced the Lovetts to put him down. Other dogs followed, including Tennyson, adopted at about age four when Guinness was five, and when Tennyson died, Bart, a rescue from Houston who arrived in early 2015. Though Bart underwent heartworm treatment in Houston, it proved unsuccessful and the Lovetts had to treat him a second time. Treatment can last weeks and the dogs have to be kept calm and quiet at home throughout—a real challenge.

"Bart would faint on exertion," Amy told me. "It was a tough road . . . but it's like with children and family: you just can't give up on them. Even if they aren't a model of what you'd expect, you learn to live with them as they are."

There have been other tough roads for the Lovetts

and their dogs, too. Tennyson had an illness that caused him to lose control over his bowels and the Lovetts spent a year cleaning up after him. Now that Guinness is old, she, too, is unable to control her bladder and her bowels. The vet bills have been formidable. When Guinness was younger and the only dog in the household, she used to run away for hours, often returning after rolling in something disgusting. But the Lovetts never quit on any of their dogs.

For the Lovetts' young daughters, Zoe and Emmery, the journey has been full of lessons as well. When Zoe turned seven she told her parents she didn't want gifts for herself, and for two years in a row she got a wish list from a local Humane Society and asked her friends to buy items on the list for the society. And when Tennyson died the girls knew they had "an opening" for another rescue dog.

"They know we are doing something special and helpful in the world," said Amy. "They know, for example, that Bo was found by the side of a road. It gives them a lot of perspective. They also have an adopted cousin, a boy, so the concept of rescue and adoption isn't foreign to them." And they know that dogs, like people, aren't perfect but that you love them just the same.

SEVERAL YEARS AGO Heather Fuqua got yet another call from dog rescuer Keri Toth. A woman heard her neighbor threaten to shoot a three-month-old puppy, since named Emily, a sheltie/collie mix, and she called Keri. Keri enlisted Heather to help and they went out to the house and saw the puppy sitting at the edge of the woods.

"We had to coax her to come out of the woods," Heather recalled. "She was sick and flea-infested and it took six months to get her healthy. I didn't intend to keep her. I loved on her, but she was scared to death of everybody. I told Keri she's too scared to be adopted out.

Dogs, like people, aren't perfect all the time. Life isn't a beach all the time for any of us. So we must savor and celebrate the moments when it is and push through the tough times when it's not. Most importantly, we must never give up on them.

It took months to get her to come willingly out of her crate.

"She's so sweet and loving, but still so scared," Heather added. "I don't know what her previous owner did to her, but the only man she'll have anything to do with is my son, and it's six years later. I just wouldn't give up on her."

SOME PEOPLE GO INTO AN ADOPTION knowing they are choosing a tough road, that there will be big obstacles to overcome, and that life with that dog isn't always going to be a beach. And some of them bring a special understanding to the task based on their own life experiences, good and bad.

I interviewed Ericka Kofkin of Jacksonville, Florida, by e-mail because she is deaf. Ericka has two rescue dogs, Avery and Zosia, both pit bull mixes, and a rescue cat, Abby Grace, who has a form of feline cerebral palsy. Ericka was supposed to be a foster for Abby Grace but multiple efforts to place her in a forever home failed. According to Ericka she's "extremely mean to anyone who isn't me."

Zosia, the most recent arrival, came to Ericka through a Jacksonville-based rescue called Pit Sisters.

"Zosia was found lying beside some railroad tracks with both back legs completely severed," Ericka wrote to me. "I was told it was horrific, bloody, and she was in extraordinary pain."

Ericka and one of the Pit Sisters, Jennifer Deane, are friends. Jen needed a name for the wounded dog and Ericka suggested Zosia. "So I was involved in her new life right from the beginning," Ericka told me. And the minute they met, Ericka knew they belonged together.

"She appears to have been trained," Ericka wrote. "She arrived house trained and knows 'down.' I suspect she also knew 'sit' and 'shake' because she reacts when I tell Avery to sit, even though without back legs Zosia can't actually do it. I asked her to 'shake,' and she attempted to lift a paw, but again, with only two legs she couldn't balance enough for a proper shake. I'm pretty sure she hasn't even noticed her legs are gone.

"Having a bipedal dog has been much more difficult than I anticipated," Ericka continued. "I get tired carrying her around sometimes. In the beginning, I struggled endlessly with her wheelchair. One day we were both so frustrated we just sat down in the front yard and had a good cry. Most doggie wheelchairs are designed for dogs with paralyzed hind legs. The legs are still there and provide counterbalance to the cart. Since Zizi [Ericka's nickname for Zosia] doesn't have any back legs, the carts aren't that comfortable for her, even though they are adjusted properly. There's a company that makes special carts for dogs without back legs, but I can't afford to get her one, and that makes me feel incompetent as her human.

"Zizi doesn't really get along with my cat," Ericka continued. "Avery and Abby Grace [the cat] *love* each other; it's beyond words really, just extremely intimate and sweet. Since Zizi can't handle being around Abby Grace, I have to lock Abby Grace in the bathroom or the dog kennel when Zizi is out of her crate. Avery likes Zizi, but Avery gets upset when I take the cat away. I am optimistic that everyone will adjust eventually. Avery and I went to watch fireworks for the Fourth of July and Zizi escaped from her kennel. The cat was angry, but all in one piece when we returned. I'm not sure how long they were out unsupervised together, but it does give me hope that Zizi's behavior towards Abby Grace comes from a place of curiosity or play rather than a commitment to eating her.

"Zizi tries my patience often," Ericka added. "When I take her out for a 'quick pee' (as opposed to a walk), I don't put her in the cart. It's too much work and she is in fact quite ambulatory without it, but she isn't that fast. If I'm hungry or running late for work, or have a big project I need to work on, or know that one of the others needs something inside, I can get a little grumbly at her slow progress, but then I turn around to check on her and see how hard she's working and all the effort in her little face and instantly melt. If I squat down and talk to her, she gives two ears up and does her best to 'run' to me. It's so precious and she always acts like I'm giving her the greatest gift in the world."

Few would argue that she isn't. Love and patience are the greatest gifts you can give to a rescue dog, especially when times get tough. And you just don't give up on them no matter how tough the times.

Teagan Sparhawk and her potcake rescues
(from left, Tia, Freckles, Simba, and Melina)

CHAPTER FIVE

Dogs Will Be Dogs

*Never did he fail to respond savagely to the chatter of
the squirrel he had first met on the blasted pine.*
—JACK LONDON

WHEN PEOPLE GET A DOG, one of the first big deci-
sions most face is what to call him or her. They'll
agonize for days, even though, unlike with children, a
dog will never have to learn to spell her name or be
teased by other dogs because of it. Albie came to us as
Albie, the name the shelter volunteer who saved him
bestowed, a name inspired, I kid you not, by a character
on the TV show *The Real Housewives of New Jersey*. He
seemed like an Albie to us, and the name was short and
cute and rolled easily off the tongue. Besides, he'd been
through so many changes already.

It wasn't *what* to call him I wrestled with; it was how
to refer to ourselves *in reference to him* that confounded
me and continues to confound me to this day. Before we
adopted Albie, I cringed whenever I heard people refer

to themselves as a dog's "mommy" or "daddy." I would think, *Really? Get a grip.* So when Albie came and I talked to him about Judy, I referred to her as, well, Judy, as in, "Hey, Albie, Judy's home!" And I referred to myself as "I," as in, "I love you, Albie," never, "Daddy loves you."

Dogs, in their dependence, are very much like young children in that regard, but it seemed to me it was anthropomorphizing them beyond all reason when people thought of themselves as "mommy" and "daddy." Yet, as anyone who has deeply loved a dog can tell you, they become an integral part of the fabric of the family, so much so that the grief when they die can be deep and profound and of a type and duration akin to losing a human family member. (See Chapter 10.) Occasionally, despite myself, I sometimes found myself referring to Judy as "mommy" when talking to Albie, but never to myself as "daddy." And I have to confess that over the years I have developed a little banter I use over and over when I am snuggling up with him that humanizes him: "He's such a good *guy*. He's the best *guy*. He's such a good *person*. He's the best *person*. I love this *guy*."

It may seem a small thing, and people will do what comes naturally to them, as they should. But how we refer to them reflects something important about how we see ourselves in relation to our dogs. And, for me, "daddy" seemed condescending, especially in light of what Albie was contributing to the relationship. Yes, he was dependent on us for everything, from what he ate to when he went out, but it felt as if Albie and I were more like dear old friends than father and child. While we all, to some extent, anthropomorphize our dogs, I didn't want to infantilize him in the process, even if I do dote on him and protect him like a precious child.

But this issue—how to refer to myself in relation to Albie—got me thinking about deeper questions about our relationships with our canine companions. As a writer I am naturally inclined to think that words matter and that the words we choose when talking about our dogs are not incidental or trivial. They say something about our connection to them and the mysteriously strong familial and deeply personal bonds we form with them. I mean, does the average owner of a turtle or a goldfish think of themselves as its "mommy" or "daddy"? (I shudder to think the answer may well be yes!) But when it comes to dogs it's very common for people to think of themselves as parents, and despite myself I started thinking that way, too. There's nothing wrong with that, per se, but before Albie came along it always struck me as over-the-top somehow.

BY THINKING OF OURSELVES as a dog's "parents," we have to be careful that we don't slip into unrealistic expectations of what our "canine children" are capable of in terms of their behavior. Dogs are domesticated animals, but we need to remember that despite our constant attempts to humanize them their genetic roots are in the wild. Yes, a dog living in your home needs to learn to live with people, and some are model household citizens. But more importantly, if you bring a dog into your home, *you need to learn to live with the dog*, including his or her wild instincts. You have to *let the dog be a dog.*

One of the main reasons a canine adoption can fail is that the humans have unrealistic expectations for what a dog will be able to do, and often when those expectations aren't met there's an impulse to write the dog off as uncontrollable, incorrigible, or just plain dense.

Can't get your dog to stop chasing squirrels? He's not stupid. He's being a dog, and dogs chase squirrels and other critters! Does he bark at strangers approaching your house? That's what many dogs do. They're being protective. Is he hoarding your shoes and piling them on his dog bed? For some dogs that's a natural way to feel close to you, especially when you're out of the house.

This isn't to say you can't or shouldn't work with a dog to curb unwanted or disruptive behaviors. The point is, dogs will be dogs, so if you want to change something that he does, do so with the understanding that your dog is doing what comes naturally to him, and if he doesn't change, it's because he probably can't. Your dog isn't being malicious or rebellious, as we commonly understand those terms. He's just being a dog.

So we, the people, have to adapt. Of course, you

don't need to let your dog drag a freshly killed rabbit carcass onto your bed or jump onto the dining room table and help himself to the Thanksgiving turkey before the family sits down to dinner. But you do have to recognize that some of what you are asking your dog to do may run contrary to what his instincts, handed down over millennia, are urging him to do. It means allowing him (or her) to indulge those instincts where it will be relatively harmless for him to do so, and not treating him like a violent felon when he does. If I'm in a position to stop Albie from destroying a small critter, a baby rabbit or a chipmunk he's pursuing, I try to do so. But on the rare occasions when he's succeeded I don't reprimand him. He's a dog, and chasing critters is as natural to him as marking trees with pee or sniffing the ground to see who else has been wandering by.* As a stray, Albie had to fend for himself in the Central Louisiana woods where those hunting instincts were essential. To expect dogs to extinguish their instincts after a few weeks or months, or even years living in a house, is like expecting the sun to rise in the west.

Paradoxically, for a dog that had to forage and fend for himself in order to eat while he was a stray, Albie has never shown much interest in "counter surfing." Countless batches of brownies, apple pies, roasts, and other hu-

---

*For an excellent read about dogs and their remarkable sense of smell, I recommend Alexandra Horowitz's 2016 book *Being a Dog: Following the Dog into a World of Smell*. It follows her other must-read for those who live with dogs, *Inside of a Dog: What Dogs See, Smell, and Know*, published in 2010.

man food have disappeared from kitchen counters across the country, plucked by clever dogs who will eat a good thing when they see it or, more to the point, smell it. Some, if they aren't large enough to reach the counter, will figure out ingenious ways to get there. They may slide a kitchen chair across the floor and climb up, or even enlist the aid of the more vertically enhanced housecat to make the quarry more accessible. YouTube is littered with such videos. It's hard not to admire the ingenuity.

Remember Noah, the dog found on a Houston scrap heap and given up for dead? As noted, one of his humans, Andrea Stewart, takes Noah and his canine sibling Sadie to work in Manhattan every day where she works as a video editor. There's a kitchen in the office with a long table and, as it happens, a surveillance camera. One day at the office the staff had set up a breakfast buffet and left the room unattended. Andrea posted the surveillance video taken a short time later on Facebook. In wanders Noah, not a person in sight. He's not a large dog, but he makes his way along the buffet table, his head tilted upward, the better to sniff the food beyond his reach. As he reaches the end of the table he finds a chair right next to it. How convenient! Next thing you know, Noah is on the table helping himself to the entire buffet. Now, here's a dog that knew unspeakable deprivation and was suffering from starvation when he was found. Can you blame him? Noah was doing what comes naturally. That's not a bad dog, or an ill-behaved dog. That's a dog being a dog, and since we humans control their access to food, that's a lot of power. Maybe dogs can be forgiven their efforts to help themselves once in a while.

I often wonder why dogs aren't driven insane by a sense of smell that is thousands of times more acute than our own. If the smell of bacon on the stove is irresistible to us (we carnivores anyway), why doesn't it drive a dog wild? Yet most dogs, if you try, can learn not to beg for food, not to stare at you from a distance of six inches while you eat, and not to snatch the roast from the dining room table. We tried, sort of, but while no roasts have been pilfered and we don't feed scraps from the dining table (well, maybe once in a while), for Albie our eating became a spectator sport and he does use his paw to signal, like Oliver Twist, that he'd like "more, sir." Having realistic expectations for a dog's behavior around food (either human-prepared or the type a dog would find in the wild) requires more than training, in my un-expert opinion; it requires an appreciation of what it means to hold the power of food—what, when, and where—in your relationship with the dog.

Of course, as mentioned, it's not just the food we pre-

> If you bring a dog into your home, you need to learn to live with the dog, including his or her wild instincts. Let the dog be a *dog*.

pare in our kitchens that will capture a dog's attention. It's the all-natural, free-range prey that scoots across our lawns and under our bushes.

When he'd been with us for just a few months, Albie spied a crippled baby squirrel that had found its way to a low-hanging tree limb in our front yard. The poor creature was clinging to the branch with its front paws, its useless hind legs dangling awkwardly in the air.

Albie was absolutely obsessed. He stood on his hind legs, extended his body as far up the tree trunk as he possibly could, leaning against the tree with his front paws. Then he ran halfway around the tree trunk and repeated the process, again and again and again. Honestly, I don't think holding a perfectly cooked prime rib in front of him would have deterred him from his singular mission.

We'd already seen him snare a mouse, a chipmunk, and a baby bunny (all of which we rescued from his maw) and, in a gross mismatch, a worm (which perished). But this situation also had all the earmarks of an unfair fight, like shooting a wild elephant from a helicopter. Nature had put the squirrel at a severe disadvantage. Were it to fall to the ground, it wouldn't have a chance. As much as I don't encourage or enjoy Albie's pursuit of critters, at least it's something of a fair fight when the critter is able-bodied, so I took the squirrel's side.

As long as that squirrel was in that tree, Albie was

going to be patrolling the base, going around and around in circles and occasionally stretching his long body as far up the tree as he possibly could, which was about three to four feet shy of where he needed to be to satisfy the urge that was driving him. The standoff continued for hours before we finally got Albie into the house for the night, where he continued to stare at the tree from the front window. I hadn't seen obsession like that since Glenn Close pursued Michael Douglas in *Fatal Attraction.*

My hope was that by morning the crippled squirrel would be gone, that he'd figure out how to work his way to the ground and drag himself to safety under cover of darkness. The next morning, I let Albie out the front door for our early walk and he bolted straight for the tree, where that poor baby squirrel remained, hanging on for dear life. Since the situation had not resolved itself naturally, it was time for some human intervention.

I found an old fishing net with a long handle, determined to give the squirrel whatever chance it might have—its handicap notwithstanding—in the great outdoors. I wasn't optimistic that a squirrel with two useless hind legs would be long for the world, but I wasn't willing to watch my very own beast of the southern wild be the end of its road. I just felt too sorry for the squirrel; in this situation *he* was the underdog, so to speak, and my rooting interest is always with the underdog.

Once it was secured in the net, I took the squirrel to

some nearby woods and liberated it there. Every single day for about two weeks thereafter, whenever we opened the front door, Albie beelined for that same tree, looking, looking, looking for a squirrel that had vanished. His persistence, the triumph of his hope over experience, was something to behold.

There are times when a dog's instincts can lead to potential trouble, *big* trouble, however. One day in the summer of 2015 I was walking with Albie and Salina, both off-leash as it turns out, at one of our regular walking places, the Bullard Woods that slope down to the northern edge of Stockbridge Bowl, also known as Lake Mahkeenac, in western Massachusetts near the cottage we used to own. By now they could both disappear for several minutes at a time without causing us undue concern. Invariably they came back, if only to check in before running off again.

They also liked to chase small critters I could rarely even get a glimpse of. Usually, when there's a small animal to be chased, they take off without warning. They see something or smell something, and in a millisecond they're off in hot pursuit. This time, however, they both just ambled off toward a clearing about fifty yards away where a few tall tree stumps stood. As I followed their path visually to the base of the tree stumps I saw what they had seen: two bear cubs making their way upward.

Surprisingly, all was silent. The dogs didn't bark and the bears didn't growl. But my first thought was, *Oh, shit*.

(That was also my second thought, but this time in all caps: *OH, SHIT!*) I took a quick 360-degree survey of the surrounding area; where there are bear cubs, a protective mother usually isn't far behind. For the moment the coast was clear, but that could change in a flash. Now I had two dogs stretching themselves as far up the tree stumps as they could as the bears slowly made their way higher and higher.

In situations like this, when a dog is in the grip of its basic instincts, it's not easy to get them to respond as you want. If it was impossible to get the dogs' attention when a mere squirrel was the quarry, surely getting them away from the bears would prove hopeless, but now there was much more at stake. I expected everything to quickly spiral out of control and looked around, fearing I would see an agitated mama bear any moment. I kept calm, but there was urgency in my voice as I called them while walking a few steps in their direction.

This wasn't Albie's first, or even second, encounter with bears in the Berkshires. On two occasions he'd chased them off from the land around our cottage. (Black bears will usually move away from confrontation. But a mama protecting her cubs might be another kettle of fish, so to speak.)

To my surprise they trotted right over to me, where I put them on their leashes and we continued quickly up the trail. But why? If it were a squirrel or rabbit I couldn't have pried them away. Yet, when I really needed them to cooperate, they did. Did they sense danger? Was there something in my own demeanor that spoke to them? Dogs can be inordinately perceptive about human emotions—call them because you just feel it's time to get in the car and go home and they may, like young kids, run in the other direction and protest. But when I called them because there was potential imminent danger, they responded immediately. I can't explain it and I don't know if they'd respond the same way again in similar circumstances. Sometimes you just desperately hope for the best.

The point is, whether you see or refer to your dogs as you would your children, or whether, like me, you have a more ambiguous approach to your relationship with them, if you want to have a successful relationship with your dogs (or any pets or animals, for that matter), it's crucial to remember that they are not human beings and cannot be expected to think, act, and behave as human beings, even young ones. (It's not unlike trying to treat very young children like full-grown adults; it rarely works to take a hard-and-fast line there.) This has nothing to do with how much, how deeply, and how well we love them. But we sell them short and may circumscribe their lives in unfortunate ways if we don't let our dogs be dogs.

To prove that point, try this little thought experiment: If those were your children who wandered off toward two bear cubs and an agitated mama bear was in sight, would you flee? I certainly wouldn't. I'd risk my life to save them, I'm sure of it, as I think most parents would. Would you do the same for your dog? Would you go so far as to risk your own life to save theirs as you would your children's? Would I have done the same for Albie and Salina as I would have for Danny and Noah? I don't know for sure, but my guess is no. Orphaning my children and making a widow of my wife to save the dogs doesn't seem like a reasonable trade-off. It's impossible to answer such questions in the abstract; we don't always act in emergencies as we think we might. But as much as I love my dogs and would do my best to save them from harm, I can't say that I'd do so if there were a good chance of losing my own life in the process.

Allowing our dogs to be dogs means reminding ourselves sometimes that, as much as we love and adore them, and as much as we want to protect them, they are, for better or worse, not children.

THE DEGREE TO WHICH we anthropomorphize our dogs can impact our ability or willingness to let them do their own doggy thing. And how we refer to them—as well as the words we use when doing so, especially in reference to ourselves—can, either subtly or overtly, determine how far we go in anthropomorphizing our dogs. At the very least, it reflects how far we have gone already. This isn't an issue of right or wrong, but simply one we should be mindful of. It is quite possible to anthropomorphize to a considerable extent and still allow a dog to live his life as a dog, provided we don't lose perspective. As long as it doesn't lead to unrealistic expectations for the dog, there seems little harm in it.

With that in mind, as I spoke with dozens of people who have a rescue dog in their lives, I was curious to know: What *is* in a name? What can we learn about a human's relationship with a dog by how they refer to themselves when talking to the dog, or about the dog? I'm not making any judgments here. A dog that has been rescued from neglect, abuse, fear, or danger deserves to be coddled, even babied. There's surely nothing wrong with that, and perhaps that's why over the past few years I have heard many, many people refer to dogs in general as "fur babies." But it's also the case that most of those I spoke with see their role as a parental one and so, not surprisingly, refer to themselves as moms and dads.

Anneliese Taylor* of Scarborough, Maine, is the mother of two young boys. When we spoke in the summer of 2016, Logan was four years old and Lucas was nine months. Anneliese adopted Tucker, an eleven-year-old Lab and boxer mix, just two weeks before she started dating her now-husband Jeff. Tucker is a Katrina dog, one of thousands of dogs evacuated from New Orleans in the aftermath of the hurricane in 2005.

*Taylor is a pseudonym. Anneliese asked that I not use her last name.

"We call him our four-legged child," Anneliese told me. "It's 'mom' and 'dad' and our parents consider them-selves his grandparents." Since Anneliese brought Tucker with her to her marriage, one of her concerns when she was expecting Logan was how Tucker would respond when she brought the baby home.

"I just didn't know how he'd feel," she told me. "My biggest worry was that he'd feel he'd been demoted." Isn't that always the worry for an older child when the second arrives?

"We had my mom bring a blanket home from the hospital and put it in his bed, hoping it would help pre-pare him, but he wouldn't go near it," added Anneliese. "My mom thought he was rejecting the baby." But those concerns proved unfounded. "Tucker took to the baby right away," added Anneliese. "He accepted him imme-diately and was on guard for him."

One winter day when Logan was two, he and Tucker were playing on a large snow mound in the backyard when people walking on a logging road behind their property came by. Tucker locked eyes on them and posi-tioned himself between Logan and the strangers until they had passed. In fact, Tucker has become so protec-tive of both children, the Taylors have to be careful when the kids are around other dogs. When a dog as-sumes the role of protector of your young children, how can you not see them as a kind of older sibling?

As I talked with rescue dog "parents" who also had children, the siblings theme was often repeated. (I suspect I'd have heard the same from those with dogs obtained from breeders or pet stores, too.) For example, Doreen Dawson of Wilmington, Massachusetts, adopted Duncan, a then-two-year-old black Lab, at the end of 2009. She and her family refer to Duncan as the "brother" of her two teenage sons, Andrew and Matty.

But some are not inclined to see it that way. Amy Lovett, whom we met earlier, doesn't view her dogs, currently Guinness and Bart, as siblings to her young daughters.

"Because our children are young [nine and six years old when we spoke], *they* are our children," Amy told me. "We don't use 'mommy' and 'daddy' with the dogs too much. They aren't my children but they are members of the family. I don't infantilize them."

No matter how intensely people love their dogs, if they had to choose, most would no doubt feel as Amy does. "If one of the kids had an allergy or a dog was a danger, our kids would come first, no question," said Amy. It's why she rightly emphasizes the importance of choosing a dog wisely.

"People need to think about a dog that really fits the household," she said. But as she acknowledges, sometimes it's not so easy. "When we got Guinness she was very challenging. Getting another dog [Bo] after three years solved that problem but I'm not sure what life would have been like if we hadn't figured it out. We stumbled into the situation."

Many of those I spoke with for this book have no human children and many acknowledge their dogs fill that role for them, much to their delight and satisfaction.

"We refer to the dogs as 'the kids,'" Elissa Altman told me. "I inadvertently find myself referring to myself as their 'dog mom.' I swore I'd never do that. Formally, I am their 'human,' but I have such a commitment to them that they are family."

> If you want to have a successful relationship with your dogs (or any pets or animals, for that matter), it's crucial to remember that they are not human beings and cannot be expected to think, act, and behave as human beings, even young ones!

AND WHAT ABOUT YOUNG CHILDREN—how do they see their dogs? As you would expect, it varies: best friend, companion, and sibling. For some, even at an early age, dogs become their world.

When I first met Teagan Sparhawk in early 2016, she was eight years old. She and her father, Brian, had come to a local library in Massachusetts to hear me give a talk about my book *Rescue Road*. Whenever I saw young children in the audience, I made a point before the talk began to speak to them and their parents. Though none of the images I used to illustrate the talk were gruesome or graphic, you can't tell the story without talking about the suffering, some intentionally inflicted, that so many rescue dogs endure, and you can't avoid talking about the high-kill shelters where so many come to an unhappy end. So I was in the habit of gently explaining beforehand that part of the story is very sad and can be tough to take, especially for young children.

I was surprised to learn that Teagan had not only read my book but was very familiar with the plight of countless dogs here in the United States and in the Bahamas. She has seven rescue dogs of her own—Hope, Freckles, Tank, Sox, Melina, Tia, and Simba—and had recently raised more than $6,000 that she donated to a rescue organization in the Bahamas she had visited, the Voiceless Dogs of Nassau, Bahamas, a feat for which the Boston Red Sox had just honored her by inviting her to throw out the first pitch at a game at Fenway Park. She told me about one of her dogs, Simba, who still bore a scar from having a hot iron placed on her back. I didn't need to worry; she'd seen worse than what I was going to describe.

Teagan is adorable. When we met she had a pixie haircut, an easy smile with big dimples, and an enthusiastic manner, especially when talking about her love of dogs. She reads countless books and startled me when she told me she was halfway through Alexandra Horowitz's *Inside of a Dog: What Dogs See, Smell, and Know,* an excellent and very sophisticated book about the mind of a dog. And she started her own rescue organization, Teagan's Treasures, which, Brian told me, would evolve as she got older. It was under the Teagan's Treasures banner that she had raised the money for the Voiceless Dogs of Nassau, Bahamas.

I was so impressed I asked her if she would be willing to speak about her work for a few minutes when I finished my talk. A little hesitantly at first, she took the microphone in front of an audience of about forty adults and began to speak about her love of dogs. With a little coaching from Brian, she talked about why rescue was so important and about the dogs she and her dad had rescued and were now living with.

Brian wasn't driving Teagan in this direction so much as taking his cues from her. Brian and his girlfriend, Kristen, adopted a rescue dog, Hope, when Teagan was five, partly to be a companion to Teagan. Hope had been tossed from a car window with three littermates when she was just three weeks old. The following year, as Teagan learned more about Hope and other dogs in need, she and her dad began caring for additional dogs, including Freckles, who came aboard as a foster but turned Brian and Teagan into "foster failures" five months later. "Foster failures," as noted, are those who intend only to keep a dog temporarily but fall so in love with their foster dog, they wind up making their home its "forever" home.

A year after adopting Hope, Teagan realized she wanted "to make a difference," said Brian, and they set up a Facebook page, the first incarnation of Teagan's Treasures, to try and educate people about pet responsibility.

"The journey for Teagan into the world of rescue began, at her choice, when she was six years old," Brian told me. The more she learned about the vast numbers of homeless dogs, the more she wanted to do, and they began taking more fosters from the Voiceless Dogs of Nassau, Bahamas, some of which they later adopted.

By age seven she was devouring books, all kinds of books, about dogs—training manuals, fiction featuring dogs, and books about specific breeds. On her Facebook page she would share posts about dogs in need, even offering her seven-year-old perspective on training and other tips, and she started raising funds by putting change jars at local businesses and selling T-shirts and sweatshirts that read "Pawtcake Refuge," a reference to the sanctuary provided by Voiceless Dogs of Nassau, Bahamas.*

---

*"Pawtcake" is a play on "potcake," the name given in the Bahamas and Turks and Caicos Islands to the feral dogs on the islands. The name comes from the caked remains of a rice-and-pea mixture common to the islands that locals would feed to the wild dogs. Potcakes are now a recognized breed in the Bahamas.

In early 2016, Teagan and Brian traveled to Nassau to see the work of Voiceless Dogs of Nassau, Bahamas, firsthand. "I knew it would be a dose of harsh reality for an eight-year-old," Brian told me, but he felt Teagan was ready. During their visit they saw maimed dogs, flea-infested dogs, and others left for dead in the streets. It was shortly after that trip that Teagan delivered the check for more than $6,000 that led to her being honored by the Boston Red Sox.

Teagan has no human siblings. Her parents are divorced and the house is crowded with kennels, dog supplies, and dogs. It's a huge undertaking. When I visited, it occurred to me that Teagan was a princess (in the best sense of the word) presiding over a real-life canine kingdom.

"Each of them would have died if we didn't adopt them," Teagan told me. "The dogs think I am one of them, but they'll never go at me the way they sometimes do with each other. When I'm home, everywhere I look there's a dog, and they jump up on me and say, *Hi!*

"I'm glad we gave each one of them a home because each one is one less dog that's loose and would have died," Teagan added. "It makes me happy to give them a life.

"It's not perfect or easy," she told me of life with seven dogs. "It's easier to have one dog. With seven it's very noisy. One time they all got sick and they all needed medicine. That was a disaster! They hated the medicine and you had to inject it into their mouths with a syringe but they all tried to spit it out. It was a mess!"

But the tough, messy moments are balanced with countless others that are sublime, including when Freckles, the senior potcake from the Bahamas, arrived and made them almost instant foster failures. "When he got here the first night," Teagan told me, "he followed me to bed and wrapped his body around my head. He was saying, *This is where I want to be.* I fell in love with him the moment I saw him.

"When I watch TV there's usually one dog on my leg and another on top of me," added Teagan. "We hold hands and this makes me realize they are home."

When Teagan goes to her mom's, Freckles goes into her bedroom looking for her. "He gets depressed and won't eat when I'm not home," Teagan added. "I miss the dogs when I'm at my mom's and they miss me."

Not surprisingly, Teagan thinks of the dogs as her brothers and sisters. "I refer to myself as 'sissy' to the dogs," she said. "Freckles is my big brother. Since I am the youngest in dog years, I'm the little sister."

Teagan dreams of having a larger kingdom someday. "I'd love to live on a ranch with a gigantic yard so I could have tons of dogs and other animals, especially dolphins," she told me.

HOWEVER WE CHOOSE TO REFER to our canine companions, we all anthropomorphize them to one degree or
another. Opinions in the scientific community vary
about what dogs know and feel and think. I am in no
position to weigh in on the science or to say with any
certainly based on my own experience how much a dog's
interior life mirrors our own. I can say with confidence
that Albie loves me because he follows me everywhere,
stares at me and seems happy when he does, looks sad
when I leave, and so on. But does he *experience* love as I
do? Is his love for me based on the same mysterious stew
of countless mental, biochemical, physical, and unknowable and immeasurable emotional and neurological
functions that come together and create the emotion we
call love? Or does he love me simply because I feed him,
speak softly to him, and rub his belly? I'm sure he'd have
"loved" anyone who gives him what I do. And, ultimately, does it really matter? The love I have for my wife
and children and other humans in my life is far more
complicated as a biochemical, psychological, and spiritual matter than my love for Albie, and, consequently,
the relationships with my wife and children are more
complicated and, in some ways, more challenging, too.
That doesn't make one type of love better than the
other, and there's no doubt the intensity of the love can

be equally deep. But equating it to love as experienced between two humans seems to me a stretch.

Which begs the question: Isn't it precisely because the nature of the love between us humans and our dogs is different that makes it so precious and appealing? I'm hardly the first person to observe that a dog's love for its humans is unconditional and simple to navigate. Dogs demand so much less of us than the people we love. They are both more patient and more forgiving and have no hidden agendas. It's *because* our relationships with our dogs are not fraught with the complications that can make human relationships so challenging that they provide such a steady stream of comfort and solace. It's fair to say they even provide a much-needed respite from our complicated human relationships, whether with spouses, significant others, coworkers, parents, in-laws, or children. I've lost count of how many people told me that one of the things they most valued in their relationship with their dogs was acceptance—nonjudgmental acceptance.

To repeat, we, the humans in these relationships, have so much power over our dogs—we decide where they will live, when they will eat, where they will walk and go on vacation, when it's time to go to the vet, and pretty much everything in their lives. We are the dominant partner in the relationship. But are we the better half?

Our dogs may like some people and not others, but

they aren't bigots. They may covet another dog's chew toy, but they are not materialistic. They may disembowel our feather pillows, but they are not malicious. They may, if they live among many other dogs, as Adrienne Finney's Guilford Gang do, assert themselves as the alpha, but they don't crave power. They may fail on occasion, but they don't let you down the way humans can. And I don't think I've ever met a narcissistic dog or one with a big ego. We may have more sophisticated brains than our canine companions, but with that sophistication comes a lot more baggage and a lot more room for error. And maybe that's why the love between a human and a dog—a domesticated creature with one paw still in the wild—can seem so much purer, so much simpler, so much more dependable, and so much less fragile. They truly are our better halves.

Callie in Pineville, Louisiana

CHAPTER SIX

Walk a Mile in Their Paws

The greatest fear dogs know is the fear that you will not
come back when you go out the door without them.
—STANLEY COREN

BY EASTER OF 2013, Albie had been with us for more than nine months, but he'd never, to my knowledge, been to a big city. The area where he'd been found in Central Louisiana is very rural, and since joining us his life had been spent almost entirely in the suburbs, with occasional trips to our summer cottage in rural western Massachusetts.

It is said that April is the cruelest month, and nowhere is that more true than in New England, when a seventy-degree day that heralds spring can be followed a day later with eight inches of heavy wet snow. On a chilly but passable spring day in April, we took Albie with us to Boston for a walking tour with my niece Annie and her then-boyfriend, now-husband, Jonah, who were visiting from Portland, Oregon. I have to admit, I had completely failed to consider that the big city might overwhelm Albie's senses.

I drove downtown separately with Albie to meet Judy, Jonah, and Annie, and pulled into an underground garage near the Theater District. As soon as he exited the car on his leash I could see Albie was anxious and frightened. Car wheels squealed as drivers made the tight turns in the garage, an occasional horn honked, and the large fans of the ventilation system, a sound I never gave a second thought to, seemed to roar. In the tight confines of the garage the noises were all amplified. Albie hunkered down low and looked this way and that, and walked that way and this, clearly looking for the fastest escape route. I managed, with much effort, to get him to the elevator, but that, too, intimidated him and he simply would not get in, nor would he enter the narrow stairwell, perhaps because he couldn't see where it ended. (Nor could I, but experience gave me faith it would eventually lead to an exit to the street.) Albie dragged me back into the garage, where I had no choice but to try and carry him, nearly eighty pounds, up the ramp. I simply couldn't get him to walk. I put both arms under his belly, scooped him up, and went up the car ramp as fast as I could, given the ungainly burden of a frightened eighty-pound dog.

When we reached the street I put Albie down. I was starting to sweat even on a chilly day. I was relieved to be out of the parking garage and into the air, and I think

Albie was, too, but all of a sudden there was all this noise—city noise, the kind we humans always expect to hear in a city—and people, so many people! Waiting at a traffic light to cross the street, we found ourselves in the middle of a group of about twenty people, with traffic rushing by from the left and the right. Crossing the street, we encountered another group of people walking toward and around us. Albie looked left and right and straight ahead as if his head were on a swivel. So many moving objects to keep track of, so many strange noises—people noises, car noises, and city noises— coming from all directions. So many new smells. And suddenly so many strangers wanting to touch him, pet him, say hello to him. So many obstacles to be avoided, and everywhere the hard surfaces of the sidewalks and streets. So little grass! It was a world so unlike the one Albie had inhabited before (except perhaps for the concrete floor of the shelter), and I had thrust it upon him without a second thought. I felt so badly for him, and some guilt for putting him in a situation that was overwhelming for him.

We met up with Judy, Jonah, and Annie, and as we made our way to the quieter streets of Beacon Hill, Albie settled down and my guilt for having thrust him unwittingly into a stressful situation started to ease. But it wouldn't be the last time I failed to anticipate Albie's reaction to a new situation.

A few months later we took Albie to a Fourth of July

party. Our friends Suzanne and Chris have a lovely beach house surrounded by spectacular gardens, and on a clear day you can see Martha's Vineyard in the distance. Because they have two black Labs of their own and welcome all dogs to their parties, we brought Albie with us. What could go wrong? At first, nothing. There were about a half dozen dogs there when we arrived. The dogs all got along fine (this was before Albie's interactions with other dogs became unpredictable) and immediately launched themselves into the salt marsh. Albie got his first ride in a convertible, during which he smiled nonstop with his face to the wind. And he got his first, very tentative taste of ocean waves. (This also predated our first trip to South Carolina.) Mostly he ran along the shoreline barking at the other dogs, all more adventurous than he. So far, so good.

But when, at dusk and without warning, someone at a house nearby set off some fireworks, all hell broke loose. Panicked, Albie looked like a soldier in World War I France trying to make it to the nearest foxhole. He moved quickly, with his body as close to the ground as he could get. He ran under tables, knocked over chairs, and eventually made his way to the safest haven he could find, the shower stall in the bathroom off the back patio. Afraid he might go into cardiac arrest—he was shaking uncontrollably—we said a quick good-bye, carried him to the car, and took off. There was nothing I could have done—I had no idea someone nearby would set off fireworks, though I suppose on the Fourth of July at the beach it's not unforeseeable—but I felt I'd let Albie down. My role, I now realized, wasn't just to care for Albie but, as best I could, be his protector, too. I may not have referred to myself as "daddy," but I sure was feeling like one. And more than anything—more than the guilt and the sadness—I felt empathy for this large but frightened creature who now depended on me to keep him safe and, as much as possible, to give him freedom from fear.

WITH CHILDREN THERE COMES A POINT when you back off because they need to learn to cope with adversity and new situations in order to become functional adults. You can't make everything in their world right all the time, especially as they leave childhood for adolescence and young adulthood. Sometimes they have to learn some tough lessons and bear the consequences. Success in life will depend in part on learning from their mistakes and overcoming their fears.

Dogs, too, need to learn to acclimate to new situations if they can, and most can learn to overcome some fears. But even as they age chronologically their need for you never wanes, and that means your empathy and compassion should never wane, either. We may feel empathy and compassion as our kids tackle the challenges of adulthood, but we sometimes hold back knowing we do them a disservice if we are always trying to ease their path. Not so with dogs. Yes, dogs mature in their own way, but you're never preparing them to leave the nest and make their own way through life. Your role as provider, protector, and nurturer remains constant throughout their lives with you because they are forever dependent. When it comes to facing the challenges of raising and caring for a dog, a healthy dose of empathy is essential.

This is true of all dogs, but when you have a rescue dog whose previous life may have involved abuse, neglect, abandonment, or some other deprivation, a dog that has beaten very, very long odds to make it to your home, there is a special poignancy to the relationship. I often feel it's my job to make up for whatever suffering Albie knew, a job that's never really done.

I may be especially soft when it comes to feeling Albie's pain. When he was stung by a bee in the Berkshires and started quivering and looked so woebegone, we rushed to a veterinarian about twenty miles away in Pittsfield. I thought he was having an allergic reaction and I wanted to do something to make it all right immediately. When I later told a friend of mine who also has dogs that we'd taken Albie to the vet, he scoffed. "For a bee sting?"

But I don't think I ever worried so much for Albie, or felt his pain so acutely, as during the days after he pulled up lame after making a tight turn running on the beach when we returned to South Carolina in the winter of

2015, this time with Salina, who had since joined the family. Almost immediately we had a health scare with each of them.

Prevailing winds and tides along this stretch of the coast sometimes wash hundreds of thousands of starfish onto the beaches, but it never occurred to us Salina would see them as a delicacy. We watched in horror as she quickly ingested several of them on our very first off-the-leash walk on the beach. Once we managed to corral her and get her inside, we hopped online to learn what we could about ingestion of starfish and started calling local veterinarians. I assumed they were toxic (and indeed some types of starfish do contain neurotoxins), but no one seemed to know or, to my surprise, to have encountered the problem before. We braced for the worst as one vet told us to be alert for any neurological symptoms. In the end (pun intended) the starfish just gave her diarrhea. But throughout our stay we simply could not bring her to the beach without her snaring a starfish at every opportunity (starfish are not great runners), and since they weren't causing her any serious distress we didn't want to restrict her to being on-leash all the time. And she was very clever: when we saw she had one in her maw we'd try and grab her and command her to "leave it," but she'd run straight into the ocean where we couldn't pursue her and would finish her snack. And two hours later, like clockwork, the expected would happen. We played this cat-and-mouse (or dog-and-starfish) game for six weeks and learned that it wasn't a threat, just an inconvenience.

But it was Albie's pulling up lame a couple of days after our arrival that proved to be the more serious problem. He was about fifty yards away and running with his usual exuberance, this time chasing Salina, who no doubt had a starfish in her mouth. She cut left and he followed but immediately fell in a heap, yelped in pain, and raised his left front paw into the air. I knew right away this was no simple sprain or thorn in his paw. I ran over to him and he looked right at me with eyes that seemed to be pleading with me.

Was it broken? Had he torn a ligament or a tendon? As I helped him up he was unable to put any weight on his left foreleg without obvious pain. He was limping badly and shaking, so I scooped him up and managed to get him into the rental house where we were staying several hundred yards up the beach.

We made a few calls and decided to make an appointment for the next day at a veterinary clinic in nearby Mount Pleasant. Albie made it upstairs for the night, limping with each step, and I did my own little amateur examination. I was able to flex his paw without any reaction from him and he even tolerated my applying a little pressure along his leg. Maybe my initial assumption was mistaken . . . maybe with a good night's rest he'd be better in the morning. Maybe it was little more than a sprain after all.

In the morning Albie hobbled to the top of the stairway. He was shaking and absolutely refused to come down the stairs. A dog's front legs bear a disproportionate share of its weight, especially going downstairs, and he obviously knew he couldn't do it. Never since he'd been with us had I seen him so sad or in so much pain and, it seemed to me, confused by what he was enduring. As I hugged him and tried to reassure him, I felt the tears well up inside me. My empathy for Albie was total. His pain became my own. I could only hope that even if my words made no literal sense to him my closeness, my tone, and my feeling for him would somehow pass directly across the language barrier and into his brain, that he would somehow take some comfort in my compassion for him.

I eventually carried him down the stairs and drove off to the vet, about twenty minutes away. The exam revealed no broken bones or torn ligaments and the vet was even able to extend Albie's shoulder and flex his paw without

When it comes to facing the challenges of raising and caring for a dog, a healthy dose of empathy is essential. Try to "walk a mile in your dog's paws," to see the world from their canine perspective, and you will be rewarded with a stronger and more trusting bond between you.

eliciting any response. There was no evidence of any catastrophic or acute injury. Rest and painkillers were advised. For weeks I'd been looking forward to watching Albie race along the beach as he had the year before (these were the days when he could mostly be trusted off-leash), and to long morning walks as the sun rose over the ocean. Now we had to make sure he didn't overextend himself too soon.

For the next few weeks I walked Albie on-leash, mostly on the sidewalks, and he limped noticeably, his head bobbing deeply up and down with each step. And with each painful step I felt a twinge of sadness for him. Perhaps to an unhealthy degree, the thought of his suffering just weighed on me. He'd survived the concrete floors of a high-kill shelter and now I wanted him to sleep on beds of roses. Perhaps most frustrating was being unable to explain to him what was happening and what we were doing to try and make him feel better. When a dog is hurting, does it have the sense, as we humans do, that things will get better? Can they imagine that they won't always feel as they do at the moment? I don't know, but I desperately wanted to assure him it wouldn't always hurt the way it did now.

It was many weeks and several X-rays later that our regular vet in Massachusetts referred us to an orthopedic specialist, where we learned Albie was suffering from advanced degenerative joint disease (arthritis) in both front legs, surprising in a dog so young. Until that sharp turn on the beach he was asymptomatic, but he had aggravated a subclinical condition. It wasn't a terrible diagnosis, but I was devastated nevertheless. He was still young and I didn't know if he'd ever be able again to enjoy the freedom of his dashes through the woods and along the beaches.

He remains on painkillers daily and at the specialist's recommendation we put him on a diet. (Less weight to bear would mean less discomfort.) He also had a series of laser treatments that warm the affected areas and are thought to provide some pain relief. Those treatments provided some comic relief, too. Everyone in the room, including the patient, has to don shaded goggles. Some dogs hate having things such as hats or glasses put on their heads and faces, but Albie, sweet Albie, is so patient. You could probably dress him up like Buzz Lightyear and he wouldn't flinch. With his long snout and big nose the goggles made him look like Snoopy flying off to fight the Red Baron.

In time his limp subsided, though it occasionally flares up for brief periods. But my fears that he would never again know the joy of running through woods or along the shore proved unfounded. Just as seeing him in pain caused me no small amount of heartache, his improvement caused me no small amount of joy.

"Walking a mile in your dog's paws" means trying to see the world through their eyes, anticipating situations that may cause them distress, and empathizing with them when they are in fear or in pain.

FOR THIS BOOK I spoke to many people with rescue dogs and, not surprisingly, found their commitment to be just as strong and their empathy just as deep, always able to walk a mile in their dogs' paws. They are very attuned to their dogs' fears, anxieties, and suffering. In some cases time and patience have helped ease those afflictions; in others the humans have altered their own lives to accommodate them. But what I heard repeatedly was compassion, understanding, and acceptance of their dogs as they were, not as one might like them to be. This is what I think of as the "rescue effect." For the most part, those who go the rescue route when finding canine companions have an underlying compassion for these underdogs and their plight. They understand that hard-luck dogs getting a second chance at life deserve their empathy.

Heather Fuqua of Pineville, Louisiana, whose second rescue dog, Emily, was a badly abused puppy, has accepted that Emily, now five, will never overcome all her fears. Emily has an older canine sister, another rescue named Callie. Emily won't walk anywhere unless she and Callie are tethered to one another by a leash.

One day Heather took the dogs to introduce them to a neighbor's livestock but all the animal noises frightened Emily terribly and she tried to drag Callie back across the street. So Heather doesn't push it; she's not determined that Emily overcome her fears, but she is determined to keep her from situations that activate them.

"When she was first picked up she cowered in the corner with her tail tucked," Heather told me. "It took her months of her being in the house with the other dogs to learn she was safe. She's been with us five years now and has made amazing progress. She is still shy, but much more willing to interact with others."

But Heather, who was widowed in 2010, knows Emily's limits and respects them. "I try not to push her into situations like that even after all these years," Heather told me about the aborted visit to the farm animals across the street. "I can't even take her to Petco because she can't handle all the noise and the people."

Heather's empathy for Emily, for all of her dogs, comes from knowing the fate that awaits countless dogs in the part of Central Louisiana where they live. "All of these babies would have had the fate of death and each has a special place in our hearts."

Henry, one of Adrienne Finney's Guilford Gang, had been abused by the man he was living with. To try to socialize him a bit, Adrienne took Henry to a local pet store. As soon as he saw a male store clerk he peed on the floor.

"He was terrified," Adrienne told me. "I hadn't expected it, but I realized right away and knew this was something we would try and work on." Some dogs will overcome such fears; some have fears that will last a lifetime. In Henry's case patience proved potent and he is now relaxed when three male friends of Adrienne's arrive at the farm for bridge night. Initially afraid of Adrienne's grown son Tim, he's now very affectionate with him.

Perhaps not surprisingly, the greatest wisdom I heard with regard to the empathy people feel for rescue dogs came from eight-year-old Teagan Sparhawk. Her father, Brian, was explaining that Freckles, one of their rescue dogs from the Bahamas, is terrified of motorcycles. "He'll bark and back away from them, but one day we took him for a walk and he went into an aggression fit towards the motorcycle," said Brian. "In rescue, especially street dogs, they've never had any sense of security, so their fears can be unexpected. You don't know their past or what they'll be afraid of. All of our potcakes are afraid of big trucks."

That's where Teagan comes in. "I go down and try to calm and reassure them," she told me. "Your dog may be scared of things a regular dog wouldn't be and you have to be ready for that. They have a reason to be fearful of certain things. They may have been hit by a truck, for example. You have to be able to comfort a dog and have patience. They won't not be scared right away. You have to take time and don't be too stern because they don't know what to do."

ONE OF THE MOST COMMON ANXIETIES in dogs is separation anxiety, and for a dog with a past, one perhaps surrendered by its owners to a shelter or just driven miles from home and dumped on a remote country road, it's no wonder. Many rescue dogs have never known human love and touch, and once they get a taste of it they never want to let go. For those who once had human families, being abandoned is confusing, bewildering, and perhaps incomprehensible. That's why that trip we made to Key West, our first time away from Albie overnight, was so difficult.

But leaving our dogs behind, whether for a few hours, a few days, or perhaps a few weeks, is difficult for most of those I spoke with for this book, with longer absences obviously more difficult than shorter ones. Most of us do it, of course, some with more aplomb than others. Some, like me, are guilt-ridden messes. I'm willing to concede this may be neurotic on my part, but it's also a function of my empathy for a dog that somewhere along the way lost a family, found another, and may harbor fears of being abandoned again. But it's how I feel when I look into those expressive eyes, especially when they seem to be saying, *Please don't go*. And once the door is closed and the painful anticipation of parting is over, the worry about how Albie is doing without me begins. I suspect the answer is that he's usually doing better with the separation than I am.

Maybe my reaction is extreme, but it's not unusual. Heather Fuqua told me her dogs handle her trips out of town well, provided her twenty-four-year-old niece comes to stay or the dogs go to a friend's house. In other words, as long as they're with people they already know.

"They're used to it, but I worry to death," Heather told me. "I worry my niece will forget something or go out for too long. It's like leaving a child for a few days. You worry. My dachshund is the worst of them all when it comes to separation anxiety. She stands by my car if she thinks I'm leaving and I have to carry her back into the house. I tell her it's going to be fine and that I'll be back. I talk to her like she's a child. You say the words, but you know they don't really understand."

When Anneliese Taylor left Tucker with her sister-in-law to take a trip to Italy with her husband, Jeff, in 2010, she was nervous. "She loved Tucker, but he was uncertain about her and she'd never had a dog before," said Anneliese. "So we were uneasy and nervous. But my sister-in-law wrote a blog, quite funny, every day or two so we could check up on them."

Our worries for our dogs when we leave reflect the feelings we have for them as we put them in a new and often unfamiliar situation. Sometimes their displeasure will be apparent when we return.

With ten dogs, Adrienne Finney doesn't leave the farm in Guilford, Vermont, often. But when her daughter married in 2016 in South Carolina she was, of course, determined to be there.

"I could either worry and feel guilty and have a terrible time or trust that everything would be okay," she told me. So she lined up sitters for the dogs and took a few rare days off from the Guilford Gang. "In hindsight, 'okay' means safe and healthy when I got home," said Adrienne.

All were safe and accounted for on Adrienne's return but there was ample evidence that everything had not been copacetic. Instead of using a gate to keep the dogs from having the run of the house, which wouldn't seem so confining, the sitters had left an unknown number of them in the TV room with the door closed.

"They ate my new leather couch—all the insides were chewed out—knocked out a door, and destroyed a storm window," Adrienne told me. "They were obviously trying to get out of the room. I don't think it was them missing me; I just don't think they were well cared-for."

And that, of course, is another worry borne of our empathy for our dogs, especially if we are leaving them in unfamiliar hands. We want them to be loved as they are when we are home, not just given food, water, and walks. We want their temporary caregivers to bring the same empathy to the task as we do, or at least something close to it. We want them to understand that some dogs may be bereft or anxious in our absence. We want them to provide not only sustenance but understanding and affection.

The question of whether to take the dogs when traveling gets even more complicated when you have more than one, and some can manage travel and some can't. Amy Lovett and her husband, Ken, don't often travel without the dogs. But on a trip to Martha's Vineyard just before I spoke with Amy in the summer of 2016 they took Bart with them but left their first rescue, Guinness (the one adopted as a puppy), because she was getting old and wouldn't have been able to manage the stairs where they were staying. "It broke our hearts," said Amy, "but it was really best for her. It's so very poignant in that way."

For some, devotion to their many dogs means no vacations for a while. Allison Smith and husband, Tom Mc-Manus, have an elderly yellow Lab, Beau, who is very sick—he takes twenty-one pills a day, needs daily physical therapy, and has one to two vet visits a week. The couple have stopped traveling for now, a testament to the empathy and devotion they bring to their life with their dogs.

When Teagan Sparhawk has to leave her home with her dad, Brian, and go to her mother's, she says good-bye and "I love you" to each of her seven dogs. "I hug and kiss each one and let them lick my face or put their paw on top of my hand," she told me. "These are our good-bye rituals. I tell them I'll be back."

AGAIN, there is no right or wrong here. Some people are more at ease leaving their dogs for a stretch than others, and some dogs will handle the separation with aplomb while others may become depressed or anxious. It's just important that we be thoughtful about how best to manage the separations, weighing both our own needs and our dogs', and do what we can to ensure their peace and comfort while we are away. As for Judy's and my own travel? The passage of time hasn't made it any easier. We might look forward to being free of the demands of caring for two dogs now (well, again, three, but we'll come to that), but we miss them when we're away and worry for them. No trip without the dogs is planned without guilt and a tinge of sadness. That said, we take them whenever we can, especially if we're going to be away for more than a couple of days. For the past three years Albie, and later Albie and Salina, happily hopped in the car for our winter break near Charleston. We yearn to go to Italy and I always balk, in part because I can't imagine leaving them for a week or ten days. Leaving a dog that has once been lost is far tougher than I ever imagined it would be.

When you have a dog and are exposing him to new experiences, or leaving him alone (especially the first few times), or trying to comfort him in times of distress, try to walk a mile in his paws. As you do, your dog will sense your love and compassion, and that itself is one of the greatest gifts you can give them.

Jason Bertrand with Sugar Mama

CHAPTER SEVEN

Keeping Things
in Perspective—
the Canine Way

The greatest pleasure of a dog is that you may make a fool of yourself with him, and not only will he not scold you, but he will make a fool of himself, too.

—SAMUEL BUTLER

IN ALBIE'S VERY FIRST DAYS WITH US, I took him to a nearby dog park a few times. Not a tree in sight, the barren, chain-link enclosure baked in the July sun. There was no place to sit and we were almost always there alone. We've been to other dog parks since, some quite nice, but I quickly developed an aversion to them. Every one was a poop-infested minefield, because not everyone is responsible, and the dynamics were too problematic.*

In those early days Albie never displayed aggression or aversion to other dogs, but as that changed and his

---

*For an amusing and insightful look at the interpersonal and intercanine dynamics of dog parks I recommend Matthew Gilbert's 2014 book *Off the Leash: A Year at the Dog Park*.

interactions with other dogs became more unpredictable (get a group of twenty dogs in an enclosed space, and the interactions, both canine and human, are going to be unpredictable) dog parks quickly fell out of favor. In the winter months, when it was otherwise closed, we headed to a golf course just a five-minute walk from our house that was open to walkers, cross-country skiers, and dogs, but there were fewer of them than at your typical dog park and there was far more room to run.

It was there, and in the woods where we walked in better weather, that I got to see and take great pleasure in the pure, uncomplicated joy that swept over Albie when he was free to run full-tilt, bound into snowdrifts, and scatter ducks on frozen ponds. Ironically, when he was a stray in Central Louisiana he was free to run, too, but without a home and people to care for him it must have been a daunting and frightening experience. Now the open spaces that were once the place where he struggled to survive were the place where he thrived. He was able to indulge his wild instincts secure in the knowledge that when he'd exhausted himself we'd walk back together to food, a warm house, and a soft bed.

Watching a dog take great joy in the simplest of things—a ball, a stick, a chase, or a snowdrift—can make you envious and get you wondering why human happiness is rarely so uncomplicated. Albie's needs were simple. Food, love, and exercise were all he needed to sustain him and make him happy. When I tossed a tennis ball for him, his world became the tennis ball. When he found a stick he liked, he carried it proudly like it was the most valuable thing in the world. When winter came and he was able, for the first time, to frolic in snow, his joy seemed as pure as the snow itself. In fact, his whole life had a simplicity and purity that only a few Buddhist monks ever seem to achieve. I loved him and I was jealous of him, too.

I SPENT THE FIRST TWENTY YEARS of parenthood trying furiously, and in vain, to keep our house clean and orderly. It didn't help that Judy isn't the most organized person. It's been an *Odd Couple* marriage with me in the part of Felix Unger (Mr. Fussy) and Judy playing the free and easy Oscar Madison. In fairness, our older son, Danny, took after me, but the younger one, Noah, would have been Felix Unger's worst nightmare. With one year left until his departure for college, I was looking forward to doing battle with only Judy standing between me and the clean, clutter-free house of my dreams.

Then, of course, we adopted a dog who, in addition to being equipped with a winning personality, shed profusely, especially in spring, left his toys all over the house, had occasional accidents, sometimes ate dinner too quickly and almost as quickly returned it on top of the carpet, brought sticks into the house and shredded them into splinters, and, despite our best efforts, occasionally bounded into the house (or the car) with paws covered in mud.

The zenith of my experience with dog messes, or the nadir, depending on how you look at it, occurred one day when I took Albie to our familiar stomping ground, the wooded trails at Elm Bank. We'd been walking for about half an hour when he bounded about twenty yards ahead of me along the trail and dipped his right shoulder toward the ground. There are scents that have an inexplicable appeal to dogs and when they find them they love to adorn themselves, much as some humans seem to bathe themselves in perfumes or colognes that are nearly as offensive. Within a matter of seconds Albie had managed to apply a lavish layer of what I still assume to have been bear scat to his neck, chest, and shoulders. It was absolutely repulsive. To make matters worse, when we returned to the car I had only a single bottle of water and a few paper towels to try and do a job that would have properly required a hazmat suit and a high-pressure fire hose. All I succeeded in doing was smearing it around and working it even more deeply into his fur. Resigned to the fact that we now had a fifteen-minute drive home in my newly vacuumed compact car to reach the bathtub—my car is almost always newly vacuumed since, as I said, I'm in the Felix Unger camp—we took off with all the windows open. It didn't help much.

I'd like to report, some five years after Albie came to

live with us, that I finally and completely let go of my need for order, but I've simply resigned myself to the extra housework and the realization that most of the rest of my life, as it always had been, will be an endless battle against the dark forces of chaos, clutter, and dirt. Still, I did have to learn to let go of some of it—my once-well-kept car is now a dirt collector, the yard will always be littered with sticks, the corners of the house a mecca for tumbleweeds made of dog fur and dust, and picking up dog poop will always be a part of my everyday routine. Having a dog forces you to look at your own foibles, neuroses, and quirks in a new light, even if you can't "shed" them completely.

IF YOU THINK BEING A NEAT FREAK and having a dog or two is a challenge, talk to Adrienne Finney, overseer of the nearly dozen Labs that comprise the Guilford Gang in Vermont.

"My house used to be house beautiful," Adrienne told me. "I was obsessive about keeping it clean. Nothing was out of place and everything had to be perfect. Well, it's not anymore. The floors are scratched, and I will get them redone, but it doesn't drive me crazy now, either. The garden isn't as well kept as it used to be, but I'd rather give these dogs quality of life than have a beautiful garden."

Most of us who are somewhat compulsive about

maintaining order know that it's an attempt to control stress at some level, mostly the stress caused by the clutter, and I, for one, marvel that there are people who can live comfortably in cluttered chaos. Dogs force you to let it go to some degree, because your need for order and cleanliness is utterly and completely irrelevant to them.

"If I'm stressed, the dogs remind me to center myself," Adrienne told me. "If I'm stressed, they're stressed. When I calm myself down, they calm themselves down. They're my reality check." And so, like Adrienne, I have tried not to sweat the small stuff like clutter and messes quite so much. Many people find that dogs fill various emotional needs. They comfort, they provide companionship and affirmation, and for some, like Adrienne, they exert a calming influence.

Anthony Everts of Staten Island, New York, would surely agree. Anthony, his wife, Valerie, their son, A.J., sixteen, and their daughter, Allison, thirteen, adopted Jada, a purebred Lab, through the P.L.U.T.O. Rescue on Staten Island in 2013. It was Anthony's first dog.

"When we got Jada I was out of work and unsure it would work out," Anthony told me. "But she's my best friend and it happened very fast. Because I wasn't working we spent a lot of time together."

The Everts then fostered several dogs and in 2015 fell in love with one of them, a Lab mix rescue from Tennessee named Cooper.

"Dogs have made me a calmer person," Anthony told

me. "I was stressed from being out of work and when we adopted Jada she calmed me. She taught me there's a lot to live for, and my family would definitely agree."

The calming influence of the dogs may be connected to what Anthony describes as "the unconditional love they have for me and that I have for them. Jada is so loyal and always wants to be with me. What I give to her I get in return one hundred percent. She understands when I've had a bad day. It's opened me up to how special the relationship with a dog can be."

If a certain degree of narcissism is fairly typical of teenagers, that, too, can be tempered by a dog. "Having the dogs has taught my kids responsibility," added Anthony. "To see how my daughter interacts with the dogs is great to watch. The kids are very involved with the dogs and they've become more compassionate because of it. A. J. is more compassionate towards them than a sixteen-year-old might be and he gets all that love back. Being involved in rescue and finding these two dogs has given us such joy and it's made me a better person."

For Allison Smith, the former Peace Corps volunteer, many of whose dogs have had Sesotho names, dogs have helped her put her general impatience

> Having a dog forces you to look at your own foibles, neuroses, and quirks in a new light, even if you can't "shed" them completely.

in perspective. "They've taught me to be a more patient person," Allison told me. "It's not their fault that they don't always get what I'm trying to teach them. The dogs you find are the ones that are there to teach you about the traits you have that aren't your best."

UNIFORMLY, people I've spoken to about their dogs talk about the perspective they've gained—about themselves and about life in general—from living with a dog. You learn, even in moments of great frustration, to laugh at yourself and, sometimes, to marvel at their ingenuity, even if it comes at your expense. More than once my dogs have made a monkey of me.

A couple of years ago we fenced in an area adjacent to our little cottage in the Berkshires. Salina had joined Albie in our household by then and they had a penchant for running off into the surrounding woods and down the hill toward the main road. And one of our wonderful neighbors was simply afraid of dogs. To ease our anxiety, and hers, we installed a fence that created an L-shaped enclosure along the front and side of the house. The deck is in front, so we looked forward to being able to relax on the deck and see the dogs without worrying about them running off in pursuit of critters. Since, as we've seen, bears are common in the Berkshires, we also thought we'd be protecting them from unwanted and potentially dangerous chance encounters.

On our first visit after the fence was complete, I was so excited to sit back and relax, worry-free. We let the dogs inside the gate. Judy went into the house to unpack some things while I went to carry some bags from the car. Then I heard Judy say, "How did Salina get in the backyard?"

I was dumbfounded. I'd just spent more than $3,000 on a new fence and somehow a fifty-eight-pound dog had escaped in less than twenty seconds. I couldn't figure out how she'd done it until she showed me. I corralled her and brought her back in and watched as she escaped again. It was so obvious I couldn't believe it hadn't occurred to me $3,000 ago.

The cottage is set on a hill and sits on concrete footings (or piers) above the ground. There is no basement. The front of the house is about four feet above grade and the back, in most places, just inches above, though on the left side it's about a foot or so. The deck, attached to the front of the house, also sits well above grade and the dogs often would take refuge from the sun by lying underneath. So I knew they had easy access to the area under the house. Yet it never occurred to me when cleverly designing a fence to keep them in that they could simply make their way under the house to the back corner, where they could get down low and out into the backyard. It was one of those smack-yourself-in-the-head moments. In retrospect it was all so obvious. My lack of foresight would soon have other unintended consequences.

I bought some sections of faux-wrought-iron fence about three feet high at Home Depot, the kind you can push a foot or so into the ground, and made sure all possible escape routes were blocked. I was feeling quite clever. The solution didn't cost much and was effective. I'd salvaged my $3,000 investment for less than $100. To celebrate I went for a bike ride. I was about twelve miles from home when my cell phone rang. It was Judy.

"We have no water in the house but there's water pouring out everywhere *under* the house." It was late on a Friday afternoon before a holiday weekend.

No one hates problems like this more than I do because I am so utterly without the knowledge, skills, or tools to fix them myself, especially when I'm twelve miles away on a bicycle. Nearly every calamity, no matter how minor, means a call to someone who can fix it and a bill, usually in the hundreds of dollars. I told Judy to turn the main water shut-off valve that sits near the end of the driveway. I now had twelve hilly miles and more than an hour to ponder what else could possibly go wrong.

When I got home, with information gleaned from Judy, and some from Barry, our plumber who extended himself to save our weekend, I pieced together what had happened. The cottage is a simple seasonal place. The hot-water heater and the pipes that carry water from the community well are all located underneath the house and are exposed. Right before the water stopped flowing to the house and started flowing out from *under* the house, Judy had seen Albie chasing Salina back and forth between the fenced-in part of the yard and under the house. Then she heard a loud bang. One of the pipes, the broken one, had never been securely bracketed to the beams above, and during the chase the dogs had obviously bumped into it, breaking it at a junction.

In the space of a few hours I went from thinking the new fence had solved a problem to realizing it had created new and expensive ones. Now the solution was beyond my shopping skills at Home Depot. We had to enclose the entire underside of the house or the mischief would continue. A couple of weeks later our carpenter, Arne, stained and installed latticework, at a cost of many hundreds of dollars, to at last create a space that would keep the dogs confined. I suppose it's a good story, and we can laugh about it now, but it was incredibly frustrating, and costly, at the time, not to mention humbling. In retrospect it was all so obvious and predictable (except perhaps for the broken pipe). But the dogs were just being dogs. They didn't care about, nor could they comprehend, the cost involved in my efforts to give them a safe space, or the subsequent expenses required to accomplish what I had thought the fence alone would achieve. I'd been outfoxed by two lovable Labs: no matter what barriers I'd put in their way, they'd found a way around them.

———

PERSPECTIVE IS A CLOSE COUSIN to humility (like the humility I experienced during the fence escapade), and when you talk to people with rescue dogs you hear a lot about how giving a hard-luck dog a home has given them perspective on their own trials and tribulations, and on life itself. Some of that perspective starts with the recognition that this dog of yours is just lucky to be alive to enjoy another day with you. When the plumbing fails, or your mechanic calls to tell you the car transmission is toast, or you've had a bad day at work, seeing that second-chance dog you love dozing contentedly by the fire reminds you of all the good things in life as well.

And when you're down or anxious or life's problems seem to be piling up, that dog's obliviousness to your earthly concerns can turn to envy. Dogs do sense when you are down or anxious or grieving, but they have no bills to pay, no jobs to stress them and take time from family and leisure, and no children or aging parents to care for and worry after. They don't fear terminal illnesses, and they never have to argue with insurance companies or figure out why the wireless router isn't working. They don't care if they're in a car stuck in traffic or about its particular make and model or whether it makes more sense to buy or lease one. They have no money concerns and they don't have to plan for retirement. (*You* are their retirement.) Politics, religion, war, and fears of terrorism don't touch their carefree lives. Sometimes it's hard not to wish that you, too, were a dog dozing by the fire and dreaming of squirrels.

BUT AS MUCH AS WE may sometimes envy their relatively carefree existence, we can learn a lot from it, too.

"When Susan and I got together in 2000 we had aging parents and a year later there was 9/11," Elissa Altman, the Newtown, Connecticut–based writer told me. "The world and the way we live in it changed. It seemed to be a struggle to live with kindness and compassion and immediacy. It now seemed that anything could happen to anyone. Our animals, especially the dogs, have taught me an enormous amount about patience and compassion when I might otherwise struggle to have it.

"My dogs don't care what people look like, or the religion they practice, or their sexual orientation," added Elissa. "We are bombarded all the time with anger, rage, and hate in the world. No matter what happens, dogs just love you. When you think of what they give back to you, love and unfettered devotion, it's a chance to understand what it means to be patient and compassionate. When I'm getting sucked into work or a political quagmire, they remind me I need to be more present. Even though I meditate, I sometimes 'fall off the cushion,' so to speak. Dogs help you get back on the cushion. They live their lives in meditation.

"For Petey [Elissa and Susan's rescue terrier mutt] it's all about love and wanting to be with you," Elissa continued. "Since Addie [their yellow Lab rescue] died, he comes and hangs out while I work and tells me when it's time for a walk. He's mindful about his days. I wish I could say the same."

Living in Newtown, Elissa and Susan were very close, physically and personally, to the incomprehensible tragedy of the Sandy Hook Elementary School massacre in 2012. So many images of that day are seared into the national memory, including a group of highly trained golden retriever therapy dogs brought in to help with the healing. If our dogs sometimes help give us perspective on bad days, events such as Newtown challenge us all to put our personal trials and tribulations in perspective.

"One of our local storekeepers, a good friend of mine, his wife was the only person in the school office who was not shot," Elissa told me. "His son, who is in his twenties and has severe autism, worked at the school and locked himself in the library. My friend didn't know for a full day if his son was okay. We are a close-knit community. One of our neighbors' kids babysat for some of the children who were killed. The community still grieves.

"We live in a society of completion," added Elissa, "where we always finish things, including grief, but people don't really operate that way. The town is still struggling. PTSD has blanketed the community and isn't budging. We'll never be the same."

In the shooting's aftermath, wherever Elissa and Susan took Addie, children flocked to her. "Her presence was so grounding and calming," said Elissa. And who wouldn't have envied a dog for not being able to comprehend or visualize the horror every citizen of Newtown was now living with?

"DOGS ARE HERE to teach us not to worry," eight-year-old Teagan Sparhawk, wise beyond her years, told me. She echoed what I heard from so many others. "They are happy with what they've got. They are in the present. They don't worry about the future. You miss the good things happening right now if you are always worried about what's going to happen after."

Angela Kretzschmar of Rye, New York, seconded that sentiment. She and her husband, Dan, have fostered more than a dozen dogs for Labs4rescue over the past six years or so. Fostering is an important but often overlooked and underappreciated piece of the rescue puzzle. Every dog that can be placed in a foster home means a rescue has room to save another from a high-kill shelter or other dire situation. And it takes special people to open up their homes and their hearts to dogs they know will be with them only temporarily. Heartbreak is part of the deal.

"Each is just as difficult to give up, but we know each time we open our home for a foster dog another is pulled from a high-kill shelter, so knowing we are saving lives makes it a tiny bit easier," Angela told me.

"The experience has made me want to be more like a dog," Angela added. "To live every moment as if it's new. If people were more like dogs the world would be a better place. They forgive and forget. They come off transport and within a few days they are changed. They don't look back; they look forward. They don't harbor resentment. People should be like this."

For Allison Smith her many dogs have provided much-needed perspective "over and over. You just can't have a bad day around Beau," she said, referring to her ailing twelve-a-half-year-old yellow Lab, adopted at age nine. "He has loved life and is simply joyous. He just makes you smile and laugh. He's so goofy, a clown in a dog suit. Even now that he's sick he's still that way. Our nine-year-old neighbor came over and he decided he couldn't just greet her with one stuffed animal in his mouth. It wasn't enough so he grabbed another. How do you not smile?"

Beau now has laryngeal paralysis that affects his breathing, and some neuropathy that has led to loss of some control over his hind legs. For unknown reasons he can barely stand on his front right leg. Despite it all he's still the happy clown he's always been. He has a little cart so the Kretzschmars can take him to his favorite places, and he still likes learning new tricks.

"He is teaching us how to handle bad things with grace and humor," said Allison. And that, ultimately, is one of a dog's great-

When the plumbing fails, or your mechanic calls to tell you the car transmission is toast, or you've had a bad day at work, seeing that second-chance dog you love dozing contentedly by the fire reminds you of all the good things in life as well.

est gifts to us humans: teaching us to try to live in the moment and, no matter what the circumstances, to do so without rancor or bitterness.

No DOG RESCUER I spoke with for this book has traveled a harder road in life than Jason Bertrand. When we first spoke he was a resident of Jacksonville Bridge in Florida. Jacksonville Bridge is a community custody facility, the last stop for Jason on a fifteen-year journey through the Florida penal system that ended just before Christmas of 2016.

Jason was born in Fall River, Massachusetts, in 1982 to two teenage drug addicts. His mother was just fifteen. His father was in prison when his mother left him, at age five, in the care of his grandmother. At age ten he went back to live with his father and his father's girl-friend, Kim, in Florida. His father was sent to prison again, and Kim, also a drug addict, tried to raise him.

First arrested when he was just eleven, Jason was in and out of halfway houses and juvenile detention facilities for the next several years. By seventeen he was serving a two-year sentence for felony battery in Florida. Unemployed after his release, he committed five armed robberies to help pay the bills.

In March 2016 he was transferred to Jacksonville Bridge to serve the balance of his mandatory fifteen-year prison term. There, Jason jumped at the chance to participate in a program called TAILS, Teaching Animals and Inmates Life Skills, run by the Jacksonville-based Pit Sisters rescue. TAILS pairs rescue dogs with inmates to train and socialize the dogs and prepare them for adoption while giving the inmates a purpose and some nonjudgmental companionship.

"I've always loved animals," Jason told me by phone from Jacksonville Bridge. "They are super-cool. But dogs are different. They are personable. I loved the idea of having a companion."

Not every inmate is approved to participate in the TAILS program.

"They want guys of good character," Jason told me, "because the welfare of the dogs is paramount. In a fire drill we have to run upstairs and get the dogs before we get out.

"There are a lot of dogs in the program and they come in a few at a time," explained Jason. "We are assigned to a professional dog trainer and a caretaker and four helpers [other inmates] who help when we are in classes. We have training books and specific objectives for the dogs. There are real goals for the dogs in terms of their behavior and they have to pass certain tests. For example, they have to be able to sit and stay while we go ten feet away and have a conversation with other people for a minute."

Jason was matched with a two-year-old pit bull named Sugar Mama, rescued from a dogfighting ring in Jacksonville. She wasn't used to fight or as a "bait" dog, a passive dog typically chained and set upon by more aggressive dogs. Rather, Sugar Mama was being bred. Nevertheless, she had two broken vertebrae that had to be surgically repaired before she entered the TAILS program. When I spoke with Jason in late summer of 2016, Sugar Mama had been with him for about six months.

Though the program aims to socialize dogs for adoption into homes, inmates whose release is imminent can apply to keep the dogs as Jason did.

"After working with her for two to two and a half months we got attached," Jason told me. "I've been in prison so long and I've never had a companion. Now I'm responsible for a living being that I care for. I can't pinpoint the date I knew, but I couldn't imagine her not staying with me."

"She's a princess," Jason said. "She won't walk on wet grass! She lies on her belly with her legs splayed out. I give her a bath every week."

Typically, once the dogs graduate from the program they are supposed to leave the facility, but Jen Deane, one of the Pit Sisters, was so taken by the bond between Jason and Sugar Mama she arranged with Jacksonville Bridge to let Sugar Mama stay with Jason until his release. Then the plan would be for Sugar Mama to go into foster care for two months with a staff member from Jacksonville Bridge while Jason looks for a job and a place to live. The Pit Sisters want the former inmates to have some stability before the dog lives with them in the outside world.

Because Sugar Mama and Jason will belong to one another they enjoy a few special privileges. Most of the dogs are being trained so they can go into adoptive homes and many people don't want dogs sleeping in their beds, so the dogs are generally not allowed on inmates' beds. Jason doesn't like the thought of Sugar Mama sleeping in a kennel every night and he can't go out and buy a dog bed, so Sugar Mama sleeps in his bed.

"She won't fall asleep in the kennel," Jason added. "Only when I bring her into the bed. Then she lays her head on my chest."

If our dogs give those of us leading relatively normal lives a sense of perspective, imagine what a dog like Sugar Mama can do for a man who has been in prison almost all of his adult life. Jason was in his early thirties when we spoke and had been in prison for fifteen years. Sugar Mama doesn't know she's in a prison or that Jason has a difficult, criminal past. That's part of what helps him.

"The [TAILS] program has given me a relief," said Jason. "On a bad day I can sit or play with Sugar Mama and she makes me smile when I don't want to. When you're depressed and with a dog it takes your mind off what you are feeling. I'm caring for something else instead of just living. I can focus on providing for something else because I am responsible for her. It's rewarding and fulfilling.

"Generally, I have a blank or angry look," Jason added. "It's a defense from being in prison for so long. When I'm with Sugar Mama people see me laugh and smile more. They see a different side of me. When you know where these dogs have come from you want to hug them, tell them, 'You won't be beat anymore, you're safe.'"

> Ultimately one of a dog's greatest gifts to us humans is teaching us to try to live in the moment and, no matter what the circumstances, to do so without rancor or bitterness.

As Jason spoke it was clear that in these hard-luck dogs, inmates like Jason see their own lives reflected. It gives them hope and purpose.

"And to see them happy after all the abuse [they've endured]," Jason told me. "If a dog can transition from being abused to happy and I've been behind bars for so long, then why can't I?" Sugar Mama has given Jason, who is apprehensive about what awaits him on the outside, reason to be optimistic and have something to look forward to once he gets out of jail. He swears he'd rather live "under a bridge" than part with Sugar Mama.

"I'm going to look for regular work, in a warehouse, maybe, and get a regular paycheck," said Jason. "I've become a phenomenal tattoo artist in prison and someday I'd like to open a tattoo parlor and get some renown for that. I'm not worried about committing any more crimes. I can't afford another day of this.

"I want to be normal and eat leisurely at a restaurant," he added. "I need to know how to navigate life. I've never had to rent a house or a car or pay a utility bill. And with all the advances in technology, how do I pay a bill electronically?"

He has much to figure out, but as he does, Sugar Mama will be by his side helping him keep perspective. And that, perhaps, is a dog's greatest gift to us, especially those lost, neglected, abandoned, and forgotten dogs whose own lives remind us that if they can overcome, so can we.

CHAPTER EIGHT

The Healing Power of Dogs

Petting, scratching, and cuddling a dog could be as soothing to the mind and heart as deep meditation and almost as good for the soul as prayer.

—DEAN KOONTZ

Thabiso, a certified therapy dog, helping a young friend

OUR FIRST YEAR WITH ALBIE, learning to live with a dog we hoped would be with us for many years to come, was also the year we prepared to send our younger son, Noah, to college.

Three years earlier, when we returned home from bringing our older son, Danny, to college at Tulane University in New Orleans, I walked into his bedroom and was unexpectedly overcome with emotion. In this room I had changed his diapers, spent countless exhausting hours rocking him to sleep, read hundreds of books aloud, and told an equal number of stories. I res-

urrected a fictional character my father used in many of
the stories he told me at bedtime when I was child:
Freddie Flunkin, a flying fish. I have no idea where the
name came from and can't recollect, more than a half
century later, a single one of the stories my father told
me about Freddie. But I suspect if I ever have advanced
dementia the one thing I will remember is that name:
Freddie Flunkin. Such are the cherished memories of
childhood; they often hinge on the smallest of things,
and when this one popped to mind it brought with it all
the warmth I felt coming from my very devoted father
and all my keen anticipation of listening to another of
Freddie's adventures.

Now Danny was eighteen, more than a thousand
miles from home, and out from under our daily gaze. It
was as if the ground under my feet had shifted. When
you go off to college yourself, get married, or have children, each of those moments feels like the beginning of
something. This, too, was the beginning of a new phase
of life but one that seemed much more like the end of
something than the beginning. I saw a huge blinking
neon sign that blared "Old Age Ahead."

When Danny went back to Tulane for his senior year,
Noah was entering his senior year of high school. We
were in transition: welcoming one, Albie, to our home
and our lives and getting ready to send the other, Noah,
off into the world.

AFTER ALL THE ANTICIPATION—the intensive college search, the decision about which school to attend, the countdown to the end of summer, and the packing—the big day arrived. We took two cars to Ithaca, New York— we needed the room for Noah's stuff . . . and for Albie.

Noah wanted to have as much time with Albie as he could, and we . . . well, in retrospect we didn't want to be driving home in an empty car to a house now empty of children. Albie was our bridge to our new life as empty nesters.

Maybe it was Albie's presence, but the raw emotion that came over me when we had returned from taking Danny to Tulane was largely absent on our return from Ithaca. Even though Judy and I would miss Noah as much as we missed his older brother, we'd also had four years of Danny being away at college to prepare for Noah's eventual departure and to come to grips with the reality that we were entering a whole new phase of our lives. Once we knew Noah was happily settled into his new life at college, we settled into our life with Albie . . . just the three of us.

When we decided to adopt Albie I didn't think much about why I had changed my mind about having a dog. Only in retrospect did I come to realize how much it had to do with the prospect of being home with no children for the first time in twenty years. So, while I didn't think of Albie as a therapy dog in any way, I suppose he really was and still is.*

Most college-age kids, boys especially, aren't great communicators while they're off at school; they're busy establishing themselves as independent young men. I didn't tell Freddie Flunkin stories to Albie, but I did talk to him a lot, just a lot of sweet nothings in his ear, and took him for long daily walks in the woods. As a bridge to our new life as empty nesters he proved sturdy and stalwart. He provided many of the pleasures of children without any of the headaches. He didn't drink or smoke pot, never totaled the car, and never asked for money. Like Mary Poppins, he was practically perfect in every way as we made the passage to this new phase in our lives. He helped fill the void left by the boys, and our daily walks gave my days a focus. His presence provided joy, demanded physical activity, and helped me feel needed.

---

*Strictly speaking, a "therapy dog" is a dog that provides affection and comfort to people who may be hospitalized or otherwise confined, or who may have suffered trauma or be suffering from emotional or psychological difficulties. To be certified as therapy dogs they must display certain traits, such as unflappability. So I'm not using the term "therapy dog" here in its formal sense. "Emotional support dogs" are like therapy dogs in that they serve similar purposes but are not certified and don't have to meet any specific criteria. By contrast, a "service dog" may, as we will see, be therapeutic for a disabled person, but it is also highly trained to help that person perform certain activities of daily living.

IT DIDN'T TAKE LONG for us to start entertaining thoughts of another dog. Albie was now, effectively, an only child, so to speak, and even though we worked at home we thought he might be lonely. Albie was still a young dog and we thought he might need something more than two "maturing" adults in his life. We certainly had room for one more, emotionally and physically, but entertaining an idea and acting on it are two different things. Truth be told, we were ambivalent. Another dog might, we feared, be more work than we were prepared to handle.

There is much to be said, and much has been written, about the life of the only child versus one with siblings. My father, who was one of eight children and saw countless children over more than forty years as a pediatrician, often said that the best-adjusted people he knew had been only children. Yet, most parents we know, including my own, opted for families with at least two children, perhaps because most had siblings themselves. There's something about the notion of having provided children with a biological or adoptive sibling to travel through life with that I, and I suspect many others, find comforting. As parents we know the odds are our children will survive us, and there is comfort in knowing they will have one another after we are gone. I know I took great comfort in my brother's presence when we went through the process of losing and grieving my parents, even though, as adolescents, we had fought ceaselessly. But it's more than giving our children a life partner of sorts; it's also about companionship (even at times of the contentious sort) in the here and now.

Many people I have spoken with have described the decision to adopt a second dog in terms of providing a canine companion for the first. It's easier to leave two dogs alone knowing they have one another for company than it is with one. When you're busy and don't have time to play, they can entertain each other. They can, simply put, be a comfort to each other. Some dogs bond deeply and become emotionally dependent on each other. Some coexist with their housemates and tolerate them. The relationships, like those of human siblings, vary greatly.

No, we weren't entirely ready for a second dog, though we'd often discussed the possibility, and we most certainly weren't prepared to raise a puppy. But with Noah off at school, when Judy and I ventured out Albie was alone at home. We kept asking ourselves the question we'd been tossing around for months: Would Albie like having an adopted sibling? Maybe we needed a therapy dog for our therapy dog. Would it be good for him? And what would it mean for us?

Part of me thought it was crazy. It had taken more

than twenty years for me to come around on the question of having a dog at all. A second dog would, I thought, complicate our lives by more than double. But to the extent we envisioned a canine companion for Albie at some undetermined future date, we imagined another young adult, one already housebroken and beyond the high-energy, chew-everything-in-sight stage. It was all idle talk; neither of us was quite ready to cross that bridge.

We had long since learned that a parent's worries never end, that even as your kids become adults new sets of concerns replace the old; once a parent, always a parent. But what I hadn't expected when I agreed to adopt a dog was that *his* sense of well-being—*his* welfare—would become such a prominent ongoing preoccupation. Perhaps because he never lost the aura of vulnerability I assigned to him when I imagined him wandering alone, or enduring month after month in a high-stress, high-kill shelter, I wanted to do the absolute best for Albie, just as I had with my kids. And as much as I worried that a second dog would overwhelm us and restrict us in even more ways than just one, I couldn't avoid thinking about what might be best for Albie, too.

SALINA WAS THE CANINE EQUIVALENT of an unplanned pregnancy. We were just entertaining the idea of a second dog, and, as noted, doing so with considerable ambivalence, when I made my first long trip with Greg Mahle while working on *Rescue Road*. Salina was one of several twelve-week-old Lab mix puppies Greg was transporting that week to a big adoption event in Rhode Island. She was exquisite, with a distinctive blue tongue (part of her genetic legacy, we later discovered; she is part chow, and chows are well known for their blue tongues) and piercing brown eyes. Because she seemed frightened on transport, instead of having her ride in a kennel in the trailer Greg let me hold her on my lap for part of the journey. And when, on our last night on the road, she wouldn't settle down to sleep in her kennel, I held her all night while she slept. By morning I was exhausted but very much attached.

Later that day in Putnam, Connecticut, a foster arranged by Mutts4rescue, the Rhode Island–based organization under whose auspices Greg was transporting her up from Louisiana, took her home for the night. The plan was for her to spend the night and to be at the adoption event the next day in Rhode Island. While I was traveling north with Greg I told Judy about Salina and e-mailed her some pictures, and we began the back-and-forth about whether we were ready for a second dog and what it would mean for Albie. Judy, who had come to pick me up in Putnam, met Salina briefly, and all night we wrestled with the question: Should we or shouldn't we?

I had felt so bereft watching her drive off with the

foster. We were going to the adoption event as part of my research for *Rescue Road*, and even when we arrived on that Sunday morning we were still wondering if we should try to adopt Salina ourselves. It wasn't even certain we could; someone could easily beat us to her. But Judy managed to find a way into the event before the gathering crowd of several hundred people and I made a beeline to the Mutts4rescue booth, found Salina, and scooped her up. We had a history together, even if it was a short one. We'd driven together from Louisiana to Connecticut and I'd held her all night just two nights before. The rest, as they say, is history.

She was one of the most adorable and lovable puppies I'd ever seen, but the first night she was with us Judy and I felt completely overwhelmed. Naturally, she had accidents in the house, she whined when left alone, and hated the crate we had borrowed. She chewed on the corners of the bedcovers and Judy's shoes. We felt trapped and thought we had signed away any semblance of the normal life we had. We were also overwhelmed by the conflicting advice in all the puppy-training books we'd quickly accumulated. For the first few nights we barely slept; not because Salina was up but because we thought we might have made a huge mistake. But we also knew there was no way we were ever going to turn our backs on the yellowish white Lab-mix puppy with the blue tongue.

In those early days Salina would lie down next to Albie and put her paws on his, and Albie appeared to beam with pride. He seemed a little befuddled by her presence but generally tolerated her and her puppy energy well. Outside, though, he sometimes played too aggressively, and she was not yet a physical match for him, so we had to monitor them carefully. We took them for walks during which Salina displayed a stubborn streak, which she still has. When she doesn't want to walk, she simply digs in. In those days we could carry her, but was she ever willful right from the get-go!

Within a week, to our great relief, she was house-trained, and gradually we started leaving the house for short periods. Maybe we could do this. Maybe life would return to normal.

Albie was never destructive—never chewed furniture or made a mess of any kind when left alone—and Salina, save for chewing the corners of those bedspreads, seemed to follow his lead. And she did the same when I took them to our favorite walking places in the woods. It takes a big leap of faith to let a puppy off the leash in the woods, but she simply followed Albie wherever he went as I fretted. They would, in time, lope through the woods, often out of sight, on separate trajectories, but in those early days it wasn't just Judy and me training her; Albie was training her, too.

Within a couple of weeks, we realized, *We can definitely do this.* There are exceptional circumstances that may require surrendering a rescue dog, but, as I said earlier, convenience, challenges, and feeling overwhelmed aren't among them: when you look into the eyes of a dog that needed a second chance it's "till death do us part."

"Are they brother and sister?" we were, and are, often asked. "Just by adoption," is our answer. But, oh, boy, were they (and *are* they) ever like human siblings in so many ways. It doesn't matter how many balls and chew toys are scattered about the house, or how many desirable sticks are lying about the yard, the only one that matters is the one the other has. Our yard is a racetrack in which Salina's speed is her only defense against Albie's superior strength; when he does catch her he quickly flips her over by grabbing the nape of her neck. As soon as he releases her she's right back nipping at his face and legs; she seems to delight in provoking him. Sometimes Albie will be lying calmly, minding his own business, and Salina will come over and wave a stick or a toy in his face or literally drop it on top of his head to get him going.

This roughhousing is a part of every day and there are times when I have to intervene to make sure it doesn't get out of hand: I grab Albie by the collar and he sits, stares at me, panting heavily, and appears genuinely torn between wanting to obey (and thereby please me) and to get back to the business of showing her who's boss (thereby pleasing *himself*).

They also compete for attention. If Albie sees me petting Salina, he comes over, sits upright, and places both paws on my arm. If Salina sees me rubbing Albie's belly, she comes over, as she does when she's hungry or wants to go out, and starts "talking"—not barking, not whining, but something that looks and sounds like she's talking! And the competition for space on our bed can be an elaborate dance in which the wily Salina often finds ways to outwit the less clever Albie, who, like Charlie Brown, always seems to believe Lucy won't pull the football away at the last moment.

Though we were completely overwhelmed at first, the three of us had soon become the four of us. Our two sons had both flown the coop, to be replaced by two more creatures that needed to be loved and nourished. They had, together, become our therapy of sorts as we made the bittersweet transition into the empty-nest phase of our lives.

When we adopted Albie, and later Salina, we felt as if we were doing them a service; after all, without adopters willing to open their homes to these dogs, what would become of them? Yes, Albie and Salina might well have found other homes and other families to love them, but more broadly we felt we were making a contribution, however modest, to the larger cause. But gradually I came to realize what they were doing for us as well.

THE THERAPEUTIC VALUE OF DOGS is well known and widely appreciated. As noted, there are certified therapy dogs that help people suffering from post-traumatic stress and other disorders, and emotional support dogs, not necessarily with special training, for people with anxiety, depression, and other mental illnesses. And there are service dogs, dogs highly trained to help those with disabilities, such as blindness, deafness, or missing limbs, navigate the world. Neither Albie nor Salina is a therapy dog in the strict sense of the term despite what they do for my sense of well-being, and they most certainly are not service dogs. But in the course of my *Rescue Road* journey I did meet a dog named Ricky who is truly both.

Ricky, a three-year-old black Lab, accompanied a woman named Ellen Leigh to a book talk I gave in the Boston area. Ellen and Ricky had been together for sixteen months at that point.

Ricky was a perfect gentleman. He helped Ellen out of her coat and sat with her quietly throughout the nearly hour-long presentation and discussion. Afterward we chatted a bit, and Ricky gave me some big doggy kisses. A few weeks later we arranged, the three of us, to have coffee together. I wanted to know more about Ellen and Ricky's life together.

I arrived first. The place was crowded and the tables were close together, but I found a table that would accommodate the three of us. Not every table was suitable, because Ellen is wheelchair-bound. Ricky is her service dog, also called an assistance dog.

In 2008 Ellen was diagnosed with mitochondrial disease, an incurable neuromuscular affliction that leaves her tired and with low energy most of the time and which can lead to life-threatening vital organ malfunction at virtually any time.

"The course of the disease can be unpredictable," she told me over coffee. "Day-to-day I don't know how I'll feel or how it will progress, so I need to limit my activity. I was hospitalized twelve times, had five surgeries, and was on a ventilator twice in the two years before I got Ricky."

Ellen met another patient in the hospital with a service dog trained by NEADS (National Education for Assistance Dog Services), also referred to as Dogs for Deaf and Disabled Americans, a nonprofit organization based in Princeton, Massachusetts. NEADS trains and provides service dogs for people with disabilities to help ease social isolation and to help with specific activities of daily living, allowing greater independence as well as companionship.

"The dog was so soothing," Ellen told me, referring to the dog she met in the hospital. "Being around the dog was like meditation. But I really didn't know if I could care for a dog, given my illness. Soon, instead of thinking about why I couldn't have a dog, I started thinking about how to make it work. I knew getting a dog was the right path even though I had some doubts."

When she left the hospital Ellen joined a conference with a NEADS representative who explained the various ways dogs can enrich the lives of people living with disabilities.

"It was one of the first times since my diagnosis that I felt hope," said Ellen. "I was excited about the possibilities, but still wondered how I would be able to take care of a dog. I didn't make an impulsive decision."

Not all dogs that enter the NEADS program end up as certified service dogs; they have to pass certain tests to ensure they are ready and able to do the job. Some, such as Ricky, come from the nonprofit organization Guiding Eyes for the Blind, which, among other things, breeds dogs that will be evaluated for their potential as service dogs. But many NEADS-trained dogs are rescues from shelters, particularly "hearing" dogs. Training can take from eighteen months to two years and many receive at least part of their training in "paws and prisoners" programs (also known as "prison pups" programs), like the one that united Jason Bertrand and Sugar Mama, to prepare them for their lives as assistance dogs. NEADS partners with nearly a dozen such programs. The process is a win-win-win situation: for the carefully screened prisoners (who work, as they do at Jacksonville Bridge where Jason was incarcerated, with professional dog trainers), for the dogs, and for the people with disabilities who eventually welcome those dogs into their lives. In many such programs the dogs spend weekdays at the prisons and weekends with "puppy raisers" who foster them and provide additional training on weekends in a more "normal" living environment, one more akin to the homes where the dogs will eventually live.

"Some train dogs specifically for the hearing-impaired," Ellen told me, "some for people with physical disabilities, some for veterans who may be disabled or struggling with PTSD, and some for kids with autism." Those who receive a dog from NEADS are expected to raise a portion of the approximately $25,000 it takes to train the dog, though combat veterans receive their dogs for free and Ricky came to live with Ellen before she'd even raised a penny. (NEADS helps recipients raise the funds; some assistance dog organizations, such as California-based Canine Companions for Independence, do not expect recipients to help defray the costs.)

"My disease has progressed over the years since my diagnosis," Ellen told me. "Ricky helps me with many tasks and gives me independence. He opens doors literally and figuratively. He's a service dog but he's also a therapy dog. He touches people's hearts, and because of that I make a connection with lots of people. People talk to me and want to know about me and Ricky. I bring Ricky everywhere I go. It was like going from a black-and-white world to color. Dogs connect you and bring out the best in people. People soften and light up around dogs."

Not only can Ricky help Ellen put her coat on and take it off—partly by pulling the sleeves up and down her arms—he can bring Ellen the phone and is trained to bark if she is in distress. If he barks when Ellen is at home, her apartment building neighbors know to call 911. Ricky is also trained to tug on a rope attached to Ellen's refrigerator to open the door and to bring her items on a designated shelf.

"I have difficulty staying hydrated," said Ellen. "Ricky can bring me a bottle of water from the fridge to my bed. He's so proud of himself when he helps me!"

Before Ricky graduated from NEADS, Ellen, like other service dog recipients, lived on the NEADS

> Whatever your troubles, dogs have a way of easing them, even if only briefly.

campus for two weeks for training and bonding. It's the culmination of an extensive process that begins with a two-hour evaluation, medical forms, and the collection of very specific information about all aspects of the adopter's life situation. Even the height of Ellen's wheelchair was recorded. Every dog shares similar baseline training, but it then needs additional training specifically tailored to its new human companion.

"Part of the training on site is how to care for your dog," Ellen told me, "including how to care for them as they age. As they get older they may not be able to do what they need to do to help you and have to retire as a service dog." If the adopter can still care for the dog they can keep it, but if they can't they have to be prepared to have NEADS arrange for another adoptive home, though a willing family member can also step in and become the dog's new caretaker, a situation that keeps the bond between the original adopter and the dog intact. "NEADS's commitment to the dog is for life," added Ellen. "It was very reassuring to be supported throughout the process. I never felt like I was in this alone.

"Ricky knows about fifty different commands," according to Ellen. "He is even trained to go to the bathroom on command." Why would a service dog be trained to do that? Because service dogs need to relieve themselves in appropriate situations and at times to go quickly and be ever ready. Some people with disabilities may not be able to spend more than very limited time in places where a dog can properly do its business, or it may need to be indoors for long stretches of time.

"Service dogs look for ways they can help their partner," Ellen told me. "Ricky is always trying to figure out what I need and how to attend to that." That's why it's important that well-meaning people who want to interact with service dogs refrain from doing so without permission: interaction can break the dog's focus by distracting it.

"Ricky steadies me, prevents falls, picks up the many things I drop, and retrieves items to help me conserve energy," said Ellen. "He helps me stay out of the hospital. Ricky loves to play and he makes each day better. Without him my life would be so much different. It's a wonderful, life-changing partnership.

"To do this I had to have faith in myself," Ellen added. "Saying yes to Ricky helped save my life! My doctors agree Ricky has improved my health, and he's renewed meaning and purpose in my life. When you're unable to work it makes you feel useless, like you're not contributing anything to the world. Ricky gives me purpose, especially when I see the ripples of happiness he sends out. He's made a difference at my church, in the building where I live, and all around my community. During my frequent visits to medical centers his wagging tail and sweet demeanor bring comfort to everyone he encounters. People are amazed at all he can do and his dedication. He opens the eyes of patients and staff to how a dog might enhance their lives, too. He brings joy to so many people!"

WHILE A SERVICE OR ASSISTANCE DOG can also be a therapy dog, therapy dogs are not necessarily also service or assistance dogs. Therapy dogs are often found at the scene of natural and other disasters to comfort those who have been traumatized, such as the golden retrievers brought to Newtown, Connecticut, after the Sandy Hook Elementary School massacre. Even dogs not specifically trained for the task, such as Elissa Altman's dog Addie, provided comfort as they walked around Newtown after the tragedy. Even in far less acute situations, dogs often provide a balm. Therapy dogs visit hospital patients, nursing home residents, and even students during exam week at some colleges to help alleviate stress.

When we adopted Albie, and later Salina, we felt as if we were doing them a service by taking them in—making a contribution, however modest, to the larger cause. But gradually I came to realize what they were doing for us as well.

But I've come to the view that almost all dogs are, or if given the chance *could be*, therapy dogs in one way or another, regardless of any specific training. Most people with dogs will attest to the calming influence dogs, such as Albie and Salina, have on their lives, in part, perhaps, because of the perspective (discussed previously) they give those of us who value them.* Why do we welcome dogs into our lives in the first place if not for their companionship and the pleasure it brings? And isn't that ultimately a form of therapy or at least a balm?

FOR ME, Albie and Salina became a way of channeling my nurturing instincts and of coping with my reluctant transition from middle-aged parent to late-middle-aged

---

*In my travels through the South for *Rescue Road* I saw far too many dogs who live lives of misery, including many who have "owners" who do not value them. I am referring here to people who love and value their dogs.

empty nester. You can't slip into senescence when you have two active canines to take care of. Recognizing the therapeutic role they were playing in my own life, I began thinking of the many ways dogs provide emotional and spiritual support to those who love them.

When he first came to us, we briefly entertained the idea of having Albie certified as a therapy dog. Our friend Chris, whose black Lab Sal visits hospital patients, is a formally certified therapy dog. But such dogs have to be unflappable. Albie was too skittish; as we learned many times, loud or sudden noises scared him. When the Fourth of July fireworks at Chris's beach house sent Albie into apoplexy, Sal was completely unfazed. That's why Sal is a certified therapy dog and Albie isn't. But Albie became a therapy dog of sorts anyway, and not just for us.

Five years before Noah left for college, my mother-in-law, Doris, and her husband of thirty years, Herb, moved from New Jersey to a senior community ten minutes from our home in Massachusetts. Both were active and, though Herb had multiple ailments, relatively healthy. But a couple of years later, at eighty-nine, he was rapidly declining. My mother-in-law, then in her mid-eighties, became his full-time caretaker and their world shrank to the confines of their apartment and the waiting rooms of multiple physicians and hospitals. In the gloom of those final months (Herb died after Noah's first semester), Albie was a consistent bright spot. Even Herb, who had become deeply depressed, would light up when Albie came to visit. Albie changed the conversation, lifted the mood, and shifted the focus. It's no wonder dogs are now used in all kinds of places and circumstances to comfort the afflicted and relieve stress—they have a way of bringing people outside themselves.

In January 2014, at Herb's memorial service, held in their apartment and attended by more than one hundred people, Albie, who would normally be unnerved by so many strangers coming and going, simply lay quietly in the hallway just outside the open apartment door. It's almost as if he knew we needed him to be on his best behavior, that something solemn had happened and he should act accordingly.

Ever since that day, whenever we visit my mother-in-law she asks us to bring Albie, and now, of course, Albie *and* Salina. She, too, had come a long way since she first learned we were getting a dog and wondered why in the world we would want to do that. Previously, I only knew from what I had read about the power of dogs to comfort and to heal; now I had seen it firsthand. It's a power most dogs have, rescue or not, but there's something especially poignant about a dog that has itself suffered some form of deprivation providing comfort to others. They have survived, even thrived, after their own suffering and remind us that we can, too.

TEAGAN SPARHAWK, the little girl I met who is devoting her young life to rescuing dogs, told me that when her father's girlfriend, Kristen, was recovering from surgery, one of her rescues, a potcake named Melina, would put her paw lightly on Kristen's stomach and then lie with her. "And when I was sick," Teagan told me, "Freckles would jump on the couch, put his butt up under my chin, and lie on top of me." Both of these dogs were lucky to be alive themselves, having come from the streets of Nassau in the Bahamas.

Teagan has also seen her dogs comfort people they didn't even know. "Kenny's is a mechanic shop near us and we bring Freckles there all the time," said Teagan. Freckles is their older Bahamian street dog with a limp from injuries suffered when a car hit him. "One day a customer came in very distraught over some family issues. She was very upset, crying and talking to Kenny in the office. We'd never met her before, but Freckles walked in while she was talking to Kenny and sat with his head in her lap for forty-five minutes."

Two of Allison Smith's dogs, Thabiso and Beau, have made more than six hundred visits as certified therapy dogs to schools and assisted-living facilities for what is called "pet therapy." (If you don't recall, Allison is the former Peace Corps volunteer who has given many of her rescue dogs Sesotho names.)

"We were at an assisted-living facility one day," Allison told me, "and there was a woman we'd never met sitting by herself. Thabiso pulled us over to her but she wouldn't respond to us. Just completely nonresponsive. Thabiso is a very big dog, a hundred thirty pounds, and he stuck his head under her arm. Still no response. But he kept nudging her hand. As we went to leave, she finally uttered one word: 'Dog.'

"On our next visit we went to her room and she told us to go away," Allison continued. "But Thabiso went in and she popped out of bed. She said nothing, but focused on him. By our third visit she was in the lobby waiting for us and she came to pet therapy every week thereafter to see Thabiso. And every week he licked her face."

For five years Thabiso has also visited the same second-grade classroom at a nearby elementary school every week. He greets every child each time and then settles on one child and remains by his or her side and won't leave. "It's always a child that's upset or has some issue going on," Allison told me. "He knows, and chooses the child who seems to need him that day.

"Sometimes he identifies a child early in the year that needs him and will kiss that child and only that child," added Allison. "He's not a natural kisser, but selective. He was born to be a therapy dog."

Dogs do seem to have an uncanny sensitivity to people who are ailing in some way. Doreen Dawson told me her love of dogs came from her father. When she adopted her black Lab mix Duncan, her dad was still living at home, but soon went to a nursing home. She last saw her father on Super Bowl Sunday of 2012, a week before he died.

"Duncan was great with my dad," Doreen told me. "He was in a hospital-style bed in the nursing home that day, and Duncan just climbed up and lay down on him. He knew just what my dad needed and wanted. *He just knew.*"

Anneliese Taylor told me a similar story about her black Lab Tucker. At family gatherings Tucker always sought out Anneliese's mother-in-law, especially at a Fourth of July barbecue in 2008.

"We just thought he always really liked Nana," Anneliese told me. "But later that fall she was diagnosed with cancer and died a few months later. Did he know? Did he have a sixth sense?"

There is a lot of research ongoing about the ability of dogs to detect various types of illnesses, including cancer, using their keen sense of smell. A 2015 story in *The New York Times*, for example, told of dogs being trained to sniff out early signs of ovarian cancer. Researchers believe dogs have the potential to smell certain chemical signatures of cancer that are otherwise undetectable. Dogs may not just be able to provide comfort to the afflicted; they may also help with diagnosis.

The capacity of dogs to comfort is connected to their uncanny ability to sense distress or discomfort and to tune in to human emotions. I heard many stories that drove this point home.

Anneliese told me that although Tucker doesn't have the personality to be a true therapy dog, he's very aware of what's happening in their family. Most people who live with dogs will attest to how tuned in dogs are to the emotions coursing through a household.

"When our boys were babies and were crying, he would come and get us and tell us we needed to do something," said Anneliese. "He also lets us know when the kids are headed into trouble. One day when Logan was very young he was headed towards an ungated stairway. Tucker knew Logan couldn't navigate it and he came and got us to keep Logan from trying to go up the stairs."

But it was in her early days with Tucker, before she was married and had children, when Tucker really changed Anneliese's life for the better. She was living in Pittsfield, Massachusetts, and working at General Electric. Pittsfield is a small city in western Massachusetts and, until recently, was down on its luck and without many young professionals.

"The young professionals would come and go every six months or so," Anneliese told me. A typical workday was seven a.m. to seven p.m. "I realized I had no strong network of friends. I only had my job, really, and a couple of friends. It became depressing. There wasn't much in Pittsfield for me. Work was demanding and I wasn't sleeping well."

Life changed when a friend persuaded her to foster, which was when she took in Tucker, the refugee from

Hurricane Katrina. She wasn't sure she could incorporate a dog into her life, given her work hours.

"But Tucker helped me get out of my shell," Anneliese told me. She was giving all of herself to her job, but Tucker helped her feel that she had "my own personal purpose again, an element of 'me.' And then we became 'us.' He added a dimension to my life I'd been missing. I became much happier and made friends walking Tucker in the neighborhood. It gave me back something I had allowed to be taken from me because I was so engulfed in my career."

Joanne Sebring of Stroudsburg, Pennsylvania, adopted a year-old black Lab named Tres from Louisiana in 2009. Tres is Spanish for "three" and Tres is missing his left front leg. He's what's known as a tripod.

"The story was his original owner ran over his leg," Joanne told me. At the time Joanne had one other dog, a yellow Lab named Lola who died at thirteen and a half in March 2016. She now lives alone with Tres and three other dogs: Roxy, a Lab-basenji mix rescued from Alabama; Ziggy, an English setter rescued from Ohio; and Buddy, a senior English setter. Buddy is a permanent foster: he'll live the rest of his life with Joanne. Because of his age he was not considered adoptable and the rescue organization that placed him with Joanne pays his medical expenses.

"The dogs know when I'm upset," Joanne told me. "Ziggy in particular will put his head on my shoulder and stare into my face when he senses I'm sad or upset, when we lost Lola, for example. Ziggy and Lola over-lapped for a year and he was missing her, too."

When Heather Fuqua's husband, Brett, died sud-denly in 2010, she and her rescued black Lab, Ox, grieved together. "Brett took Ox everywhere," Heather told me. "And all of a sudden Brett's gone. He just didn't know where Brett had gone." The Fuquas also had two other rescues at the time, Emily and Callie. "The three of them stayed close by me," Heather added. "They sensed my grief."

Nancy Allen-Ziemski, the Norwich, Connecticut, vi-olinist who has fostered more than thirty rescue dogs since she adopted her rescued Lab Rosco in 2009, echoed what Heather told me.

"In 2011 I lost one of my best friends," Nancy told me. "He lived in Idaho and died five days after heart bypass surgery. I wasn't able to be there and it was a very difficult time.

"Rosco let me cry for half a day and was on my lap kissing and licking me," Nancy added. "He was there to comfort me and did the same when my dad died in 2012. He let me be inconsolable for a while, then decided enough is enough: Mom doesn't need to cry anymore. Dogs are very in tune with our feelings. They know when we're upset and are along for the ride. I don't feel right not being with a dog. I'm not as calm or relaxed."

One of Adrienne Finney's many dogs, Lila, often visits nursing home patients, where, according to Adrienne, "she's a big hit and loves to sit there and be beautiful." Adrienne is the "matriarch" of Vermont's Guilford Gang. But it's the entire Guilford Gang, whose daily lives Adrienne chronicles on Facebook with stunning photographs, that seem to provide a form of online therapy for the nearly one thousand people who follow her there. Adrienne's followers get to know each of the brood intimately, and the various relationships that have formed among them.

"So many people are drawn to this gang of dogs," Adrienne told me. "People are attracted to the fact that there are so many and that they get along so well. They never fight and rarely even growl at each other. They know each other so well that when I throw a ball they know who will get it and the others will back off, like baseball players. There's no food aggression and each has his or her own spot." The Guilford Gang suggests the kind of amity and community many of us would aspire to. "I think people follow us on Facebook because these animals who were all going to die are living in harmony together," added Adrienne.

NOT EVERYONE LIKES DOGS, of course, and not all dogs are likable. But just watch the faces of people who encounter a friendly dog, and far more often than not you'll see a small glimpse of the power of a dog to lift human spirits. It would be unfair to expect a dog, no matter how loving, to cure all that ails us. But surely the simplicity and purity of a dog's love, its innocence, its seeming inability to form ulterior motives, its unwavering devotion, and its willingness to accept us as we are, not as we or others would wish us to be, are part and parcel of what makes our relationship with them therapeutic. They bring out the best in us (most of us, anyway) because they tap into our compassion and the better angels of our nature. Dogs are the most forgiving of creatures. Not all will be able to overcome the troubles of their past, if, as many rescue dogs have, they've endured abuse, neglect, or trauma. But the vast majority will learn to trust people, even if they have been betrayed by them before. They bear no grudge. I have seen pit bulls living their lives chained to a stake in a barren and blisteringly hot yard in Texas greet a rescue volunteer with a wagging tail and lavish kisses, happy for a moment of human touch. And I've seen dogs in a high-kill shelter in Louisiana, as Albie once was, strain to make contact with a single finger reaching through the kennel bars toward them.

Whatever your troubles, dogs have a way of easing them, even if only briefly. That's the healing power of a dog.

CHAPTER NINE

Finding the Four-Pawed Fountain of Youth

The dog was created specially for children. He is the god of frolic. —HENRY WARD BEECHER

Duncan

IT IS ONE THE IRONIES of having children that they can certainly make you feel old. Our eldest, Danny, was, as a baby, hands down the worst sleeper ever. He just never seemed able to slip quietly into a slumber, at least not at night when for our own sanity we most needed him to get some shut-eye. You could rub his back for hours and he'd still be awake. You could play quiet music, talk in gentle tones to him, or, as he got a little older, read stories to him endlessly, and he just wouldn't go to sleep even as we were ready to collapse, fully clothed, wherever we happened to be at the moment. Many nights, when he was an infant, after hours of effort he'd fall asleep holding my finger pushed through the slats in his crib. But no matter how gently I tried to extract my finger from his grip he'd wake up and cry and we'd have to try all over from the beginning. Some nights I'd tiptoe as quietly as I could to his bedroom door trying to make my escape, and a floorboard would creak, undoing in less than a second what it had taken me hours to accomplish. So, mainly because of fatigue, having young children often made me feel old—old and very tired.

Back-to-school nights, parent-teacher conferences, PTA meetings, sports leagues, practices (whether music or sports), the long car trips to New Jersey to see Grandma and Grandpa, playdates, birthday parties, visits to zoos and parks and movies of negligible interest to adults (with some notable exceptions, especially *Toy Story*) . . . anyone with a child knows the drill. Life with children forces you to grow up, be an adult, and to put the interests of others, your children, before your own. It makes you realize the carefree days of your youth are over. This isn't to say they aren't replaced by something else, something wonderful and meaningful, something even better,

> Dogs, with the laughter, perspective, and physical activity that caring for them brings, can keep us feeling younger—physically, mentally, and at heart.

or why would we bother? It's just that being young with children can sometimes make you feel old and very grown up with grown-up responsibilities.

As I said earlier, if you think your parental responsibilities and worries end when the kids go off to college, or even after they graduate, in most cases you would be wrong. And so even being an empty nester is no guarantee that you can, however briefly, reclaim the freedom that you knew in your youth before children. But I found that Albie often made me feel young, and still does, even though I know we are marching into old age together.

WHEN DANNY HAD GRADUATED FROM COLLEGE and Noah was a college freshman, we wasted no time using our newfound freedom to do something we weren't able to before. That's when Judy, Albie, and I took off from Boston by car and headed to South Carolina for the month of March in 2014, the first of our three winter respites there.

Albie loved the snow. Watching him exult in a couple of feet of freshly fallen, pure white fluffy snow, and hunt for a tennis ball I'd thrown and which had disappeared somewhere in that ocean of white, was delightful. Snow seems to energize dogs. But Judy and I always hated winter in New England and, since our work was portable and the kids weren't living with us, we were no longer bound to home. The beach on Isle of Palms, about twenty minutes from Charleston, is dog-friendly and we had friends with a second home there, so that's where we went.

We left on a bitterly cold day. When we stopped for lunch in northern New Jersey, in my hometown of Paramus, we took Albie to a nearby dog park for a break. The ground was covered in ice and frozen snow about two feet thick and it was still bitterly cold. We lasted about two minutes, hustled back to the car, and felt like we were escaping from some inhospitable and dreary planet. By the next afternoon, we spotted some daffodils in bloom in North Carolina and, a little farther south, just north of the South Carolina border, our first palmetto tree. Both were sights for winter-weary eyes used to a visual palette of shades of gray and white. Late the following afternoon, we watched Albie take off after some sea birds on a barrier island beach awash in golden late afternoon sunshine. I was wearing shorts.

The older folks who migrate south along Interstate 95 for the winter and return north in spring are known as snowbirds, and I found it hard to accept that that's what we'd become. How long would it be until we were eating dinner at five p.m. to take advantage of the "early bird specials"? The nest was empty and here we were, joining all the white-haired seniors fleeing south for the winter.

While we were in Charleston that first year I wrote

the book proposal for *Rescue Road*. Albie had changed our lives in so many ways and I adored him so much that he inspired me to try to shine a light on the countless dogs like him in need of "forever" homes. Knowing the need was great, I wanted to encourage people thinking about getting a dog to consider a rescue dog and to dispel the myths, many of which I had once believed, that often discourage people from adopting a rescue or shelter dog. Two years earlier I had, with some trepidation and after years of objection, agreed to get a dog. Now I was about to devote myself full-time to telling his story and those of thousands like him by writing *Rescue Road*. Maybe this was Albie's purpose—he was a messenger with a story to tell, but he needed help telling it.

In his early days with us, when we walked the trails along the Charles River, I had a profound sense of well-being. As I watched Albie, a southern dog, experience his first snow a few months later, I shared his excitement. But walking that beach on a mild winter day with Albie, and watching his pure joy and exuberance as he splashed along the water's edge chasing seabirds he would never come close to catching, I noticed another feeling—I felt young again, and liberated. Liberated from the claustrophobia of winter, when darkness closes in early and every restaurant, coffee shop, and movie theater is clogged with bulky winter coats on the backs of every chair and the floors are gritty and wet from people trekking in from outside. Claustrophobia from the aftermath of big snowstorms, when you shovel paths a foot wide to get to your car, spend an hour clearing it of snow and ice, to drive on roads clogged with snow to half their normal width, and walk like a rat in a maze for weeks on end to get anywhere. Claustrophobia from being holed up at home for days at a time except to get the dogs out to do their business. But it wasn't just the change of scenery and the weather that made me feel younger and more alive. Stepping onto a wide sandy beach aglow in late afternoon sun and watching our spirited Albie run to his heart's content was liberating; I felt an extra spring in my own step. In some ways being at the beach with Albie was like having a young kid again, but without the same demands and the lack of sleep, and far less complicated.

Joanne Sebring, the woman from Stroudsburg, Pennsylvania, who adopted three-legged Tres (now Trace) from Louisiana in 2009, is sixty-five. Trace arrived in Pennsylvania during a blizzard. Unlike most rescue dogs, Trace was driven north by his foster, who was on her way from Louisiana to Massachusetts to visit family.

"There was at least a foot of snow on the ground," Joanne told me, "and it was coming down fast." Because Joanne lives on a mountaintop, she drove into town to meet Trace and his foster in her truck. "When I arrived, southern boy Trace was romping in his first snow, making it fly here and there, eating it as fast as he could, and greeted me with a hug."

With four dogs now—Trace, Roxy, Ziggy, and Buddy—Joanne says the dogs keep her busy and "feeling young.

"I have to keep up my energy level to care for them," she told me. "They make me exercise."

Joanne sent me a short ode she wrote that reflects the youthful spirit that life with dogs can inspire:

Trace, my funny, loveable boy, teaches me—
Be cheerful in the face of adversity
When you fall down, shake yourself off and get back up
  again
Snuggle every chance you get
Find the JOY in everything!
Meet the day with enthusiasm

Enthusiasm. Is there anything that reflects the sensation of feeling young more than greeting each dawn with enthusiasm?

FOR ANNALIESE TAYLOR, the mother of two young children, Tucker, their black Lab, doesn't so much make her feel younger (she's only in her thirties, after all) as he makes her feel "in the present, alive, and aware of the moment. If you are really interacting and appreciating your dog, you are in the moment, too," she told me. For those of us who have a few decades on Anneliese, that sounds very much like a description of what it is like to be young.

The Guilford Gang's head honcho, Adrienne Finney, is about my age: sixty-something. "Physical activity is part of it," Adrienne told me. "But it's also the relative simplicity of their minds." Having such a large brood keeps Adrienne mentally fit.

"I get out of my head and into theirs," she told me. "There's a purity in relating to them that makes me feel youthful. They make me laugh and they keep my mind active because I am managing ten personalities. I have to be alert to what each is doing and redirect them if necessary. Considering all this keeps my mind busy like a schoolteacher's, and I used to be a preschool teacher. Even the older dogs are like kids."

For Doreen Dawson, fifty-four, her black Lab Duncan keeps her physically active *and* young at heart. "I move more because of Duncan," she told me. "Having him forces me to walk every day. The playfulness, the goofiness, and the romping around keep me young. In the pool he uses the ladder and it's so much fun to see him enjoying life."

"The fact that I have to get up, walk them, and interact with them keeps me going and active," Heather Fuqua of Pineville, Louisiana, told me of her three rescues. "I have a responsibility to them. They keep you from feeing old because you have to focus on *them*. They keep you from giving up when you're down. And they keep me laughing with their antics."

These were themes I heard over and over, talking with people with rescue dogs—the laughter, the perspective, and the physical activity keeping people feeling younger physically, mentally, and at heart. And while most people with dogs, rescued or not, would probably express these same sentiments, knowing a dog had previously suffered some form of deprivation, or had been languishing on death row in a shelter somewhere, only heightens the meaningfulness and the pleasure of watching them and sharing in their joy and love of life.

There is indeed deep pleasure in watching the joy of a dog that once was lost, but now is found and has been given a second chance at life. And Albie in all his youthful enthusiasm made me feel young again, too. Not spring-break young, but young enough. A dog will do that for you.

Beau and the Beau-mobile

CHAPTER TEN

Lives Well Lived

Dogs' lives are too short. Their only fault, really.
—AGNES SLIGH TURNBULL

H OW DID I not see this coming? From the time I first started thinking about this book, and all through the process of writing the book proposal, it never occurred to me to write about the inevitable. Even if we adopt them as a puppy, a dog's time with us will be relatively brief, which makes each moment we have with them all the more precious. Much as we might wish for it, our dogs won't live forever.

Albie, as we've just seen, was helping me feel young again. He slowed my life down enough to start appreciating many of the small details that can get swept away as we rush through our busy lives, often missing what makes life worth living to begin with. I paid more attention than usual to autumn colors and to the smells of the woods. I slowed down to enjoy watching him roll over and over and over in the snow. He helped me to live more on Albie time—walking farther and longer on the beach in South Carolina than I might have otherwise. There were times when I'd be working and he'd just sit and stare at me until I took the time to rub his belly. If too much time went by without my turning my attention to him I'd feel him pawing my thigh until I closed my laptop. And I stopped long enough at times just to lock eyes with him and wonder what he was making of his own life.

When Albie and I lie together and stare at each other as I stroke his head, kiss him on the side of his face, and whisper sweet nothings into his ear, I often have the sense that inside Albie's head, and perhaps inside every dog's, lies the answers to all of life's eternal mysteries. I sometimes think there is some universal wisdom floating in his head, just inches away from mine, but utterly inaccessible and unknowable. When we are face-to-face with a dog I wonder if we are tantalizingly close to revelation but just have no way of getting inside. And every dog takes those answers with him or her when they leave us, as someday they must.

"SOMEONE RECENTLY TOLD ME that bringing a dog or cat or other animal into your life is a contract with sadness," Elissa Altman told me when we spoke in the summer of 2016. She and her partner, Susan, had just lost Addie, adopted when Addie was about seven. She was just shy of fifteen when she died.

"Anyone who has watched an animal age doesn't want to make the life/death decision," Elissa said. "But they are dependent on us to give them lives of peace and happiness and safety, and part of that is making sure their departure is one of peace and safety, too."

The subject came up in the very first interview I did for this book with Staicey Scholtz of Vermillion, Ohio, who, it will be remembered, adopted Jake, an eleven-and-a-half-year-old yellow Lab who had lived the first ten years of his life chained in a small yard behind a trailer home never knowing a moment's joy. He had just eight months with Staicey and her husband, Brad, when he was diagnosed with osteosarcoma, an aggressive cancer. Jake had suffered so much in his life, and Staicey and Brad wanted to be sure they helped Jake pass before the inevitable pain set in. After a life of suffering, Jake, however briefly, knew love.

Staicey's story—Jake's, really—hit home, and it hit hard. From the moment he came into our lives and I contemplated growing old with Albie, in some small corner of my mind I feared what it would be like to lose him. And the more people I spoke with, the more I heard stories of loss that had shaken people to the core and brought forth deep grief. Elissa Altman was certainly right when she told me that for all the joy they bring us in life, loving an animal is also a contract with sadness.

> Even if we adopt them as a puppy, a dog's time with us will be relatively brief, which makes each moment we have with them all the more precious.

Before Albie, I knew in some abstract way that losing a dog was, for its human companions, a true and profound loss. After all, people say the dog is "a member of the family" all the time. When I was a kid we lost two dogs, one to an accident and another to natural causes. But I still didn't, as an adult, quite understand the depth of the grief that so often accompanies the loss of a dog. I figured it meant a few days or weeks of some sadness, but it could hardly compare, so I thought, to the grief that accompanies the loss of a parent, a loved one, or a human friend. Yet I eventually came to realize that this isn't necessarily true. Dogs, cats, horses—animals of all types—often become wonderfully and inexplicably integral parts of our lives and our families, and losing them can be devastating.

When Reilly, the dog we cared for one weekend and who helped break my opposition to a dog of our own, died, our friends Anne Marie and Dave struggled to come to terms. He'd been with them since he was a puppy. For months Reilly's dog bed with his favorite toys remained in their living room and his leash hung in its familiar place. They just couldn't bear to put them away and they felt, and still feel, Reilly's absence acutely, every day. For some the best way to honor a dog's memory is to get another. For many devoted to rescue, the best way to honor a dog's memory is to *save* another.

JODY PROCT OF NORWALK, CONNECTICUT, lost Chloe, a rescued Lab she adopted when Chloe was twelve. Remarkably, Chloe lived another five years and died in 2012. For a couple of years Jody wasn't ready for another dog, but she'd been a Labs4rescue volunteer for several years and in 2016 she reached out to Keri Toth in Louisiana, looking for another senior. She ended up adopting Magnolia, a four year-old (not quite a senior) found in a junkyard near Alexandria, Louisiana, with six nursing puppies. Magnolia also had an untreated leg injury that eventually required that the leg be amputated. "Having a dog with special needs is fine with me," Jody told me. For many, such as Jody, welcoming another second chance dog into their lives is a way of coping with the grief of a dog that has passed.

For Dave and Anne Marie, though, Reilly was simply irreplaceable, and more than a year later the loss still stung.

WHEN I SPOKE WITH ELISSA ALTMAN, who had recently lost Addie, the wounds were even fresher. "When Addie became ill and had trouble breathing," Elissa told me, "I slept in bed with her with her head in my arms. When we made the decision to let her go I knew I'd be heart-broken, but I didn't know *how* devastating it would be. I could hardly speak for a week. I almost couldn't function. I had deadlines but I had to let myself fall apart."

Elissa and Susan's other rescue dog, Petey, had, for five years, only known life with Addie. "He always looked to Addie for confidence and social cues," Elissa said. "He fell into a horrible depression." Months later, Petey was just coming out of it. Even Elissa's mother, who didn't live with Addie, fell apart.

"She was a huge presence," said Elissa. "She was an intensely kind and compassionate animal."

DOGS, LIKE PEOPLE, get old and sick and die, and that is a part of adopting a dog we often don't think about at the beginning. Most of us will outlive our dogs, which means we will be their caregivers not only when they are young and spry and relatively healthy, but as they age and become infirm, too. It's part of the deal.

It is a testament to the meaning of a dog's life, and the role dogs play in our lives, that he or she is so deeply mourned by those who cared for and loved him (or her) and who were repaid in spades. Vast numbers of dogs in this country and around the world die lonely, painful, anonymous deaths without so much as a name, and it is from such a fate that each dog rescued by a loving family is spared. But we know when we surrender our heart to a dog and take great joy in each of our days with him or her, that one day there will pain to bear and grief to endure. But death is part of life for all living things—as Buddhism teaches us, without suffering there is no joy, without left there is no right, without darkness there is no light, and without death there is no life. As hard as it can be at the end, who would regret all the years of love and pleasure that came before?

REMEMBER BEAU, Allison Smith's dog with laryngeal paralysis and neuropathy that affected his breathing and control of his back legs? The one that despite all his ailments, twenty-one pills a day, physical therapy, and two vet visits a week was still the class clown?

"Beau's illness is very difficult and challenging," Allison told me in the summer of 2016. "There are days when my husband comes home and I say, 'You need to take over,' and I'm in tears. The logistics of his illness are great and the cost is astronomical."

"There's a saying that 'you never get more than you can handle,'" added Allison. "I am the right person for these dogs [the Smiths currently have four] because I have the time and experience. I would trade for a healthy dog, of course, but their illnesses are part of them and part of what makes them who they are. They didn't choose to be sick, so you don't give up on them."

In early November 2016, just as I was getting ready to

submit this manuscript to my publisher, I received a heart-wrenching e-mail from Allison: "We had to say good-bye to Beau on October 6th," she wrote. "It seems like just yesterday . . . He was part of a Labrador Health Study at Cornell so we brought his body there for necropsy as part of their research. They found two additional diseases we were all unaware of. He also had Degenerative Myelopathy [an incurable, progressive disease of the canine spinal cord that is similar in many ways to amyotrophic lateral sclerosis], as well as a very rare form of lung cancer. He continues to give as they are now studying these things and he is part of their Biobank where any researcher can get his info. His DNA also went to the University of Wisconsin, Madison, for their genetic study on laryngeal paralysis in Labs and Goldens. We are trying to make something positive come of his loss. It was so difficult as he was still so mentally present, but the disease just robbed his body of its ability to function.

"We did all we could to make Beau's last weeks wonderful for him," Allison added. "He could no longer go on walks so we got him a 'Beau-mobile' beach cart and were able to go for 'walks' to his favorite spots. He had lots of visits from family, lots of treats, and worked on learning new tricks. His last ones were counting to five and resting his chin in my palm. Beau loved snow (or as we refer to it 'Sneau'). After the lack of sneau last winter, we could not let Beau leave this life without his sneau.

We made arrangements with RPI [Rensselaer Polytechnic Institute] to go and load a pick-up truck with their Zamboni sneau [from the hockey rink] just for Beau. It was wonderful to see him in his sneau pile that we got on Friday, September 30th, and somehow managed to make it last until we had the home euthanasia vet come on October 6th. We said good-bye to Beau outside on his sneau pile . . . We miss him fiercely."

Reading Allison's e-mail brought a mix of emotions. There was, of course, the incredible poignancy of it all and the sobering reminder that someday we would have to say good-bye to Albie and Salina. Allison's love for Beau and her heartache were very palpable. But Beau's story, even at the end, was so affirming and uplifting, too. We bring these dogs into our lives not just because their antics bring us pleasure and we enjoy their company and patting their heads. We do it because it makes us more compassionate, thoughtful people, because it affirms our humanity, and because by making their lives better we better our own. And when the time comes to ease their passage we are tested to be at our most selfless—to put their comfort and peace above our own.

KELLY THOMPSON OF BRANFORD, CONNECTICUT, whose dogs Maci and Estelle became instant friends when Estelle joined the family in 2013, told me a story that seemed to epitomize all that is right and true and meaningful about giving a dog a second chance at life, even when, *or especially when*, that life is cut short. Those who described their dogs' last moments to me, as Staicey, Allison, and Kelly did, always did so in ways that re-created an agonizingly sad but somehow lovely moment.

"Maci was our first rescue and came from Texas," Kelly told me. "When she'd been with us for about two years we decided maybe she needed a 'fur sibling,' as she seemed to miss us and her two human siblings when we were at work and school."

Maci was a Labs4rescue dog, and so the Thompsons started looking online at other adoptable dogs available through Labs4rescue. That's how they found Estelle, a yellow Lab from Louisiana who, like so many southern rescue dogs, was heartworm-positive.

Like our Albie, Estelle was found wandering the back roads of rural Louisiana. "It appeared she had had multiple litters of puppies," Kelly told me. The short video showed a timid, gentle dog, and the Thompsons decided to adopt her.

"Her arrival date was changed twice because her heartworm load was so heavy," Kelly told me. In April 2013, finally heartworm-negative, she was on her way north.

"We brought Estelle to our vet within a day or two," Kelly continued. "She was about six to eight years old. She had a pellet lodged in her belly. Her teeth had been cut or filed down to prevent her from chewing through ropes or chains, and we suspect she may have been used as a bait dog because of her sweet demeanor. And because of the heartworm she had bad scar tissue around her heart. Our vet wasn't optimistic and recommended we see a cardiologist.*

"We were not financially ready for a dog that needed a two-thousand-dollar cardiologist visit," Kelly told me. "We were a family of two working parents with two young children living paycheck to paycheck. But having anticipated Estelle's arrival and upon meeting her and having her in our house for only a week or two, we had fallen in love."

Sadly, the cardiologist confirmed their worst fears. Estelle's heart was badly damaged and she was likely to live just another six months or so.

"We were devastated," said Kelly. "We spoke to our children on the way home and told them through tears that it didn't matter how much time we had left with her. We wanted to show her what having a family who loved her felt like, and that is what we did."

With the help of their vet and "some pretty costly meds" that Kelly's husband, Gregory, called "our car payment," Estelle lived a happy and active life for another year and a half.

---

*I know from personal experience that Labs4rescue works hard to ensure the health of every dog it puts up for adoption, or to make sure known health problems are disclosed to potential adopters. But it's not a perfect science, and the Thompsons understood that.

Even when they got the bad news, there was no question in Kelly's mind that they would keep Estelle and love her.

"But we were preparing right at the outset for her eventual death," said Kelly. "We were trying to make our family more complete, but here we were. I thought, this is so unfair to our family, but we will love her and teach our children to love her more nevertheless.

We bring dogs into our lives not just because we enjoy their company and patting their heads, but because it makes us more compassionate, thoughtful people, it affirms our humanity, and because by making their lives better, we better our own as well.

"It was very difficult at first," added Kelly. "But once we decided as a family to show her the best life she could have, we stopped focusing on her death and focused on her life. Sometimes she would pass out chasing Maci, and the children would run to her side. We'd put our hands on her and reassure her and she'd get back up and then lay down. Estelle didn't know her limitations and she would just stop and fall over. But our children and their friends learned compassion by caring for Estelle.

"She loved Maci and she helped us welcome our first foster failure, Brody," Kelly continued. "She spent many happy days in our backyard and at the beach."

In the early fall of 2015 Kelly noticed Estelle wasn't jumping down from the bed. A day or two later she wouldn't go up the stairs. She was sleeping a lot.

"I made a vet appointment for Sunday," Kelly told me, "but forty-five minutes later I didn't think we could wait. She just didn't look right. An X-ray showed a growth of some kind and our primary vet told us to bring her in the next morning."

Estelle had a tumor that was at risk of rupture. The vet advised she not go home because if the tumor ruptured there it would be traumatic for the children.

"But they allowed us to take her for one hour and to pick up the kids at school so we could have a picnic on the front porch with Estelle," said Kelly. "She ate chicken and cheese and laid on the front porch with us and Maci and Brody, and then we had to say good-bye.

"We lost her on October fifth, 2015," Kelly continued. "We miss her terribly but know what we showed her more love in her last year on earth than she received in her many previous years. She knew that we would do anything for her. We all felt so good that Estelle knew what it was like to be completely loved and completely content. She didn't have to worry about anything. She was safe and warm and we gave her one and a half years, more than expected. If we'd had to say good-bye after one or two months I'm not sure she'd have known she ever had a home and was loved unconditionally. That made it easier to let her go.

"The fact that she knew she had a home confirmed how wonderful it was to have her with us, whether for twelve days or twelve months," added Kelly. "Having creatures that can't talk has taught our children compassion that has carried over into life in general.

"It's so meaningful to give a dog near the end of life love and comfort, especially dogs that have suffered or who, like Estelle, had such an awful life before," Kelly said. "It makes you want to set their world right and to let them know that they didn't deserve what happened to them and that they are worthy of all we give them.

"I now have a special place in my heart for seniors and would love to be a foster or adoptive home for dogs that need hospicelike care in the future because I feel so strongly about the need to show these beautiful creatures the love they so genuinely give to us," Kelly concluded. "We gave Estelle so much, but she gave us so much in return."

WHEN HEATHER FUQUA'S DAUGHTER Addyson was just two, they had a foster failure named Bones. Heather knew Bones had had a family before; he had good manners and knew several commands. Bones was about eight and, like Estelle and so many other southern dogs, heartworm-positive. A few years ago Heather returned from a cruise to find Bones ailing and laboring to breathe. The verdict from the vet was that he was in heart failure from the heartworm disease. One night, Heather and little Addyson lay down to sleep with Bones, and when they woke up he was dead. Heather was heartbroken but concerned for Addyson. The death of a dog or other pet is often a young child's first experience with the impermanence of life.

"Bones loved Addyson," Heather told me. "He was right with her everywhere she went and protected her from bugs and snakes. She crawled all over him and loved on him and he just thought that was heaven." It no doubt was.

"Addyson cried, of course," added Heather, "but I assured her that Bones would always be with her." Such words are often uttered to comfort the grieving, but they are true. Those who have touched our lives, whether human or animal, remain with us long after their physical presence has ceased.

AMY LOVETT, the woman who adopted a rescue dog named Bo to be a companion for her rescued Lab Guinness, still going strong fifteen years after the Lovetts adopted her as a puppy, related the story of Bo's death in 2004.

Bo had stopped eating and the Lovetts didn't know why. They took him to the vet, hoping, of course, they'd find the cause and that it wouldn't be serious. As they moved through the medical process and waited for test results, they became "more focused on knowing it's serious," said Amy. When they learned Bo had lymphoma, their first question was, "Can we do something?"

The Lovetts were referred to a veterinary oncologist.

"This vet wouldn't look us in the eye," Amy told me. "He didn't have a great demeanor. But a lot of vets won't say what they would do if it were their dog. Most say, 'It's up to you.' But we asked him what he would do. He said, 'He's suffering and I would decide to end his suffering.'

"Despite his weirdness, the door had cracked and we were grateful he'd said this," said Amy.

"The thought of waiting through the weekend so we could go back to our regular vet was too much," said Amy. "He'd had the last best day of his life and we asked the oncologist if he would help."

Bo was "Amy's dog" more than Guinness.

"I said, 'Okay, buddy, thank you for everything,' and he lay his head in my lap. He knew. There are always second thoughts, but we had looked into his eyes and saw something that told us he was ready. We would have spent the money and taken a loan if necessary, but the doctor said this was end-stage lymphoma and we just couldn't put him through any more suffering.

"The worst part was leaving his body with the vet in Oneonta," added Amy. "We had nowhere to bury him, so I felt as if we abandoned him there. Guinness stopped eating afterwards and we knew she needed another buddy and soon after adopted again."

Amy's story made me realize that deciding to let go is the hardest decision of all, for it requires self-lessness at precisely that moment when the heart-ache and impending sense of loss will be most in-tense. And Amy's precise words were exactly the

I don't know for sure, but I doubt dogs can contemplate their mortality as we do (both our own and theirs), and perhaps that's why they are so capable of living in the moment.

words that had come to me almost fifteen years ago while staring down the barrel of my own mortality in a recovery room after surgery for thyroid cancer. I was in extreme discomfort, but knew my prognosis was good. But, I asked myself, would I be willing to endure all this if it were not? That's when I had an epiphany—it would be preferable to leave this life "on my last best day," just as Bo did. That thought will be with me if and when we have to make a similar decision about Albie or Salina.

When I look back at the photographs we saw of Albie online, the photographs that told us Albie was "the one," I see a younger dog. Day-to-day Albie has always looked the same to me. But there was a day about a year or so ago when I noticed his muzzle looked just a little bit whiter and the little tufts of fur around his ears a little bit flatter than I remembered. He can still chase Salina with exuberance (she's always been a step or two faster than he is) but with a little less endurance. Thankfully, he seems little bothered by his arthritis. But in the five years he's been with us he's aged the human equivalent of two to three decades. He was a veritable teenager when he arrived from Louisiana, but just a few years later he's now well into middle age. Yet, perhaps because of his past as a stray and a survivor of a high-kill shelter, he's always been something of an old soul.

In our dogs we can see the trajectory of life condensed into a relative handful of years. In little more than a decade they are born, pass through infancy, childhood, adolescence, young adulthood, middle age, and eventually old age. At whatever age we welcome them into our lives, the chances are high we will see them through their final days, and in so doing are reminded that, as George Harrison wrote, "all things must pass."

The hair around my temples was gray four years ago when Albie came to us and now he's catching up to me. In a couple of years, right around the time I'm signing up for Medicare, we'll be at roughly the same stage of life, and then he will pass me. It will fall to Judy and me in the not-too-distant future to, as Elissa Altman said, make sure his departure, like his life, "is one of peace and safety, too." Perhaps this all sounds maudlin, and I don't dwell on it on a daily basis, but the more I spoke with rescue dog adopters, the more I realized it is part and parcel of the rescue experience.

I don't know for sure, but I doubt dogs can contemplate their mortality as we do (both our own and theirs), and perhaps that's why they are so capable of living in the moment. Dogs don't make plans for tomorrow or next week or next year. They don't set long-term goals. They are liberated from so much that weighs on us humans. Aware of our own mortality, we often encourage ourselves and others to do the same with clichés: enjoy every moment, live like there's no tomorrow, seize the day, life is short, and so on. Dwelling on one's own mortality is no way to live, but we are blessed or cursed with the knowledge that someday we will no longer be here. And that means we must all, at some point, contemplate our own demise. The same is true when we think about the dogs that, just by being themselves, bring us so much joy. It's why we are willing to make what Elissa Altman called that "contract with sadness."

The Guilford Gang

CHAPTER ELEVEN

Come On, Get Up, It's a New Day!

Dogs . . . leave paw prints on our lives and our souls,
which are as unique as fingerprints in every way.
—ASHLY LORENZANA

IT WOULD HAVE BEEN LOGICAL, I suppose, to close this book with the last chapter about the death of a dog. But it would also be highly unfair to all the dogs whose stories have been shared here and to all of their human companions who shared their experiences, wisdom, and advice, to end this book that way. Because, for all the pain at the end of the road, the journey itself is what matters most, and in that journey there is great love, empathy, joy, and caring, even at the sad, and sometimes bittersweet, end. To discourage people from adopting dogs because of the sadness that ensues when they reach the end of their lives would deprive humans and dogs alike of a truly sublime and rewarding relationship that can last years and bring great happiness and comfort.

I make no apologies for being a strong advocate for

adopting a rescue dog. However, I try to avoid that swamp of ill-feeling between those who support adopting rescues versus breeders and other advocates of pure-bred dogs. In the dog world there is a lot of friction between the two camps, but my personal approach is to each his or her own. I know many wonderful dogs who came from breeders, and wonderful people who live with purebred dogs, and that's fine. I have no doubt that the bonds are just as strong, the love just as great, and the journey just as joyful. Rather, my advocacy for adopting a rescue or shelter dog comes from a more practical and broad perspective: With hundreds of thousands of deserving dogs (and perhaps far more than that) looking for a forever home in the United States alone, and continual proof that dogs who are given a second chance at life make wonderful companions, it would be hard for me personally to justify getting a dog any other way. And, as I've noted elsewhere in this book, it makes the experience of living with a dog all the more poignant and rewarding when you know that dog has beaten very, very long and seemingly impossible odds to get the chance to be wrapped in your arms, or run through Christmas snow or freshly cut grass, or jump exuberantly into a lake or pond.

For me, watching Albie slowly come to feel safe in our home, and to declare himself home when he took his leap of faith to jump onto our bed to sleep after weeks of sleeping under the coffee table in the living room, was sublime. Knowing we helped save his life, and Salina's, has given added meaning to the whole experience and made every moment we share together (well, *almost* every moment!) a special gift, for them and for us. Rare is the time when I look at Albie curled up in one of his favorite sleeping spots and don't think of where he's been and the long, hard road he had to travel to reach us and to find his home. Perhaps because Salina was such a young puppy when we adopted her, and we know she never suffered, the feeling is less intense when I think of her, but I love her, too. She went directly from the home where she was born into the hands of caring rescuers and then literally into my arms on Greg Mahle's truck. But she, too, could easily have become one of the countless dogs born into this world never to have a name or to know love or kindness. But for a quick-thinking and compassionate young man in rural Louisiana named C. J. Nash, Salina and her littermates could easily have ended up at the local pound to have their lives extinguished just days after they were born. It was C. J. who reached out to a local rescuer rather than bring the puppies to the local pound as his father had asked.

As young Teagan Sparhawk put it to me, "If you get a dog from a breeder, it's just a random dog. It's not in danger. The dogs in the Bahamas [where Teagan's rescue work is focused] are *dying*. There they treat the dogs as pests instead of pets."

And that, in a nutshell, is the case for a rescue dog.

———

Too often, myths and misconceptions about rescue or shelter dogs scare people away. When my wife, Judy, first suggested a rescue dog, I harbored some of them, as noted earlier. But several veterinarians I've spoken with are quick to dispel the myths that rescue dogs are generally less healthy, less behaviorally predictable, or somehow damaged beyond repair.

"Over the years my clients have become much more savvy about rescue dogs," Barbara Hopey told me. Barbara is a retired veterinarian from eastern Massachusetts who still owns a veterinary clinic. "We see a lot of them now. People will pay fifteen hundred dollars [or more] for a pure breed and the dog comes in sick [to its first appointment]." And purebred dogs can be genetically predisposed to certain ailments. Bulldogs are prone to pneumonia, for example, and golden retrievers to hip dysplasia and some types of cancer. New research suggests that more than sixty percent of goldens, one of the most popular breeds in the country, will die of cancer—not just be diagnosed with cancer, but die from it.

Many people think buying from a breeder is the best way to ensure they are getting a healthy dog with a good temperament. "There's no guarantee if you go through a breeder," Barb added. "So many are puppy-mill dogs. If you are buying a dog long-distance it's likely from a puppy mill. I've seen good, reputable breeders do all kinds of checks but there are no guarantees. The puppy's parents may be OFA-certified [certified by the Orthopedic Foundation for Animals that their hips are healthy, because hip dysplasia can lead to chronic pain and other problems] but that doesn't mean their puppies are okay.

"In our practice we see more sickness with bred dogs than rescue dogs," Barb added. Other vets I've spoken with have had the same experience, though there are still others who disagree. Perhaps it's just the ratio of rescue versus bred dogs in their patient populations that leads to these differing views. But the point is that there's no clear evidence that bred dogs are healthier or have fewer behavioral issues than rescue dogs.

In her *New York Times* bestselling book *Inside of a Dog: What Dogs See, Smell, and Know,* canine cognition expert Alexandra Horowitz makes no bones about it. She argues that mixed breeds tend to be physically

It makes the experience of living with a dog all the more poignant and rewarding when you know that dog has beaten very long and seemingly impossible odds to get the chance to be wrapped in your arms, or run through snow or freshly cut grass, or jump exuberantly into a lake or pond.

healthier dogs and of more even temperament. The best breed, she says, is a mixed breed.

ONE OF BARB HOPEY'S MANY DOGS, most of which are rescues, is Noelle. Like Noah, Andrea Stewart and Linda Zalkeskie's rescue dog, Noelle was found in Melrose Park in Houston, and her story parallels Noah's in many ways. Erin Bouton, a local rescue volunteer, found her lying on the street in January 2015 and thought she was dead. When she approached she was shocked to see Noelle was still breathing. Erin took Noelle to a nearby animal hospital and contacted Kathy Wetmore of Houston Shaggy Dog Rescue, who also helped save Noah and found him a home with Andrea and Linda.

As she often does in such situations, Kathy wrote about Noelle on her Facebook page, and that post, another by a second volunteer, and Barb Hopey's response help illuminate the urgency with which so much rescue work is done and the heart that goes into it from one end of the rescue chain to the other.

"We were able to bring in another dog from Melrose Park yesterday," wrote Kathy Wetmore. "Erin picked her up and took her to the Aldine Animal Hospital for us. Sadly it may have been too late for this girl. She is in critical condition at the vet's and they are trying to stabilize her. She bled out during the night and is close to dying. Praying they can pull her through. She was in the exact same location as Noah was found and Erin said there are about five more dogs they are trying to rescue in similar condition from that location. It's just so sad these dogs have been thrown out and neglected for so long and no one that lives in the area cares because they just pass them by. I am heading to Aldine this morning and will update on her condition later. We are calling her Noelle . . . thank you, Erin, for getting her off the street."

Shortly after Erin took Noelle to Aldine Animal Hospital, another local volunteer posted a picture of Noelle lying broken and nearly lifeless on the street, looking almost like a large baby bird that had fallen from its nest, the way her front legs were curled up and her head was lying flat on the pavement.

"This picture is worth more than a thousand words, especially when it comes to animal cruelty and neglect," she wrote. "This is Noelle. She was found (picked up yesterday) in a park KNOWN for dumped dogs, discarded with ropes or chains around their necks, sometimes already dead, severe mange, starvation . . . the list goes on and on. This girl—and a few others lately—have been found with motor oil all over the body; an uneducated or 'old school' way of an attempt to cure mange. This dog is anemic, has swollen legs, emaciated and has demodex mange . . . Melrose Park is ACROSS THE STREET FROM HARRIS COUNTY ANIMAL SHELTER! This has been in the media, they have been told numerous times about this issue, yet the City of

Houston does nothing. Houston, we have a serious problem! Please share her story, 'like' the Shaggy Dog Rescue [Facebook] page to follow her (hopeful) improvement, donate to this or your favorite shelter or rescue, advocate, volunteer . . . whatever you feel is in your heart to do to stop this madness."

Barb saw that post the same day it went up and she decided to do everything she could to help Noelle. With no intention of adopting her, she donated to help cover the costs of her hospitalization and, as Noelle started to improve, her spay and heartworm treatment as well. Over the next several months Noelle made a complete recovery. Kathy told Barb she thought Noelle should come to live with Barb and she agreed.

On June 24, 2015, six months after being left for dead, Noelle arrived in New England. Today, Noelle lives with Barb and many canine companions in Massachusetts and is, in Barb's words, "a cherished family member." For Noelle, like Noah and so many others, it's a new day.

AS IS SURELY abundantly clear by now, it's the knowledge that you've saved a dog from a desperate situation, from neglect or abuse or certain death, that magnifies and deepens and sweetens the relationship that's forged between the adopter and the dog. But it's hardly a one-way street, as so many people I spoke with would attest. A rescue dog will repay your love and kindness over and over again.

When Brett Fuqua, Heather's husband, died suddenly in 2010, Heather kept fostering dogs in her Louisiana home to keep herself busy. But her rescue dogs, both adopted and fostered, did more than keep her busy; they gave her, she told me, "a reason to get up and get out of the house.

"You need to take care of them and train them," said Heather. "I've had full-grown Labs that were severely underweight, and to see them get healthy and being loved and showing them that they can trust again gives you a sense of deep accomplishment. This was an important part of helping me through the grief. The process of getting these death row dogs back to health is so meaningful. You see these dogs dumped on the street or at the pound and know these are the ones that need love.

"You can go down any dirt road here and see dogs that are hungry," added Heather. "Then you see them do a one-eighty and you know you've saved a soul. That's what makes rescue dogs the best."

THERE CONTINUE TO BE many small moments in our lives with Albie and Salina that, with the passage of time, I tend to take for granted but which are really quite precious, even in their repetition. Some are the smallest of moments, but I know I will miss them when the dogs are no longer here to create them day after day.

What is almost always the worst moment of my day is immediately followed by the best. I could easily sleep until at least eight every morning (I am *not* a morning person), but sometime between five-thirty and six-fifteen a.m. I hear it: either Albie or Salina, whoever has been aced out of sleeping in our bed that night (and they rarely both sleep in our bed together), walking toward the bedroom, nails click-clacking on the wood floor, a sound that always rouses the other. Then there are the morning shakes to get the cobwebs out, which always makes their dog tags jangle.

For a moment I hope against hope they will just go back to sleep. But I know better. I crack one eye open and there are two faces inches from mine telling me it's time to get up and let them out, time to have breakfast, time to start the new day. If I don't start moving right away, which is always, there is usually a low grumble from Albie. Then they'll both start pawing me gently. Sometimes Albie will sit up by the side of the bed, put both paws on my arm, and stare at me intently.

That first moment of awareness, the realization that my sleep will be interrupted for the umpteenth morning in a row, is the worst moment. Looking into their eyes and knowing they need me to get the new day rolling is the best.

And why do I do it over and over and over again, even when I know that in a few minutes I'll be outside so they can do their business and it's below zero and the wind is whipping snow in my face? Because every morning Albie and Salina bring me the eggs—those eggs Woody Allen talked about in *Annie Hall*. Because they need me to do certain things for them they can't do for themselves, like open the door and fill their bowls with breakfast. Because I feel good knowing they are both lucky to be alive, that we have given them a chance to indulge their doggy-ness, that they feel safe and secure in our home. And because they make me feel needed in the most fundamental way. They have made me a nurturer again.

Life, of course, is a long string of moments—some good, some bad, some happy and some sad, some exciting and some dull—most of which we never savor as they rush by until, before we know it, those moments become days, the days become weeks, then months, and then years. The years, too, accumulate, and before we know it we've passed our halfway point ten or twenty years ago, but are still feeling there's so much left to do, to experience, to stop and enjoy. Time is the most inexorable of forces, the inescapable leveler of the human experience, and the great humbler of our ambitions as we race to squeeze more out of whatever time we have. Dogs, however, seem to exist outside of time even though we watch them age. For that reason they provide some respite from the unavoidable and somewhat melancholy reality that even as our lives get longer with each passing day, our time grows shorter. All things must pass, yes, but that's what makes the moments precious . . . they are, ultimately, an ever-dwindling commodity and, therefore, all the more valuable with each passing day.

It's not solely those early morning moments when Albie and Salina stare at me expectantly that I treasure. I also love watching them chase balls and unseen forest creatures and compete for possession of a simple stick. I love the enthusiasm with which they greet me every time I walk through the door.

I love watching them eat crunchy treats, too: the way they chew with their mouths open to one side reminds me of the legendary actor Jimmy Cagney talking with a cigar in his mouth. And I love watching Salina take her position lying at the top of the stairs that lead from our kitchen to a game room above the garage so she can survey her domain below. She looks so regal up there.

I love watching Albie, all eighty pounds of him, curl up in a dog bed made for a puppy a quarter his size. Albie even has different ways of lying down, some of which, to me, seem especially sweet and which evoke a more powerful, protective instinct in me. When he's curled into a tight ball his eyes usually have a more worried look (I could be projecting, but who knows?), one that seems to cry out for me to provide some physical and verbal comfort. Those moments have special resonance because they remind me of his vulnerability and dependence. Other times, when he's gotten too amped up tussling with Salina, for example, and I separate them, he lies uneasily on the floor like the Sphinx—head erect and alert, panting hard, and trying, it seems, to compose himself even though you can tell it's taking every ounce of his willpower not to pounce on her again. I have to smile as I watch him apparently trying to decide whether to stay where he is and please us, or pile on Salina again, which would be much more fun.

Albie and Salina aren't what is known as a bonded pair; they don't stick to each other like glue and don't seem outwardly dependent on one another. They don't sleep next to one another for comfort. They don't go looking for each other in the house. When they play, as I've said, it tends to get pretty rough at times, though mostly it's Salina outrunning Albie back and forth across the yard in a game of *catch me if you can*. And when he does get her cornered—against a fence or behind some bushes—you'd be forgiven for thinking they're fighting. Albie growls and barks and sometimes takes her down by the scruff of the neck, his larger, more powerful body atop hers as she struggles to right herself, escape, and start the chase all over again. It might seem like Albie is the instigator because he seems more aggressive, but she typically gets it started and eggs him on, even after multiple takedowns.

But when we go somewhere by car with them, on our long drives to South Carolina, for example, they spend their time in the backseat lying down with her head resting gently on top of his, both with their eyes closed, a scene so sweet and lovely you'd never imagine they are ever any other way with each other. Salina, ever the mischief-maker, the little princess, has a different persona in the car—she seems more docile, more uncertain, and more dependent on Albie for comfort. In the car he seems very much the older brother and she the kid sister. How they know not to mix it up in the car, I have no idea; we didn't have to train them on how to travel safely and quietly in the car, they just did it from the start.

Of course, there are many moments that repeat themselves every day or week that I could do without. The insane barking whenever the UPS man or the FedEx deliverywoman approaches the front door, or one of the flocks of wild turkeys that live in our neighborhood decides to graze on our lawn. It's enough to drive you absolutely crazy. There's Salina's favorite habit of denuding trunks of hemlocks and other shrubs of the branches she can reach, and there are holes dug in the garden in pursuit of small creatures unseen but apparently easily smelled by a dog's hypersensitive nose. And, of course, every day I have to pick up poop piles. Does anyone enjoy that?

IN MY EXPERIENCE, losing a human loved one focuses you on the very small details that made them unique. The

way my father hung his pants from the top drawer of his
dresser, for example, or the way he used to do his taxes
on the dining room table using a large sheet of examin-
ing room paper from his office for the meticulous calcu-
lations he made in a neat hand by pencil, or the unique
way he whistled every time he came home to announce
his arrival, a two-note whistle I can re-create today
from hearing it many thousands of times during my
childhood. The way my mom always tore a piece of gum
in half before giving it to us. I suspect it will be the
same with Albie when he's gone—the way he circled
very precisely before doing his business, the exact way
he tilted his head when I asked him a question, the look
in his eyes when thunder and lightning were exciting
his nervous system and scaring him, and, of course,
those early morning gazes from a distance of a few
inches.

With that in mind, as I spoke to people who had a
rescue dog in their lives, I was curious to know if there
were moments, even ones that seemed pedestrian, that
recurred in their lives with their dogs that they especially savored, moments like my early morning gaze into
the expectant eyes of Albie and Salina. Because when
they are gone those are the moments we will miss the
most, the ones that in their absence will remind us of
how much their presence filled our lives.

"At nine thirty p.m. Duncan is ready for bed," Doreen Dawson told me. "He gets annoyed if we aren't

ready and lets us know by snorting. In the morning he waits for the first toe to hit the floor and as soon as it does he's ready for the day! He sticks to me like glue and I love his little cues about going to sleep and getting up in the morning."

For Joanne Sebring, the human who belongs to three-legged Trace and three other rescue dogs, her sublime moment is in the evening when, after a busy day, she finally plops herself down on the couch. All four dogs join her, two on either side.

Anneliese Taylor and her family have three special moments every day with eleven-year-old Tucker. Every morning Tucker, no matter what else is happening in their busy household with two young children, insists on a belly rub. "He'll get us to stop whatever it is we are doing, roll over, and wait for us to rub his belly," Anneliese told me. "In the evening, when it's story time for the kids, he goes and gets his stuffed animal and brings it into [four-year-old] Logan's room, lies down, and waits for the stories to begin," she added. "If there's no story that night you can see the disappointment on his face." When story time is over (or if it's been skipped) Tucker always has dessert with Anneliese's husband, Jeff. He gets a Yoghünd, a yogurt-based treat formulated especially for dogs, while Jeff has something sweet made for human consumption. Tucker is getting on in years, so the little rituals they enjoy and cherish today will no doubt be among the vivid memories of Tucker they will have when his time comes.*

"My favorite time of day is in the morning before we get up," Debbie DeWolfe of Ashland, Massachusetts, told me about her rescue dog Bess, a small black Lab from New Orleans that came north in 2012. "Bess belly-crawls right up to me, sticks her nose under my arm, and just snuggles for a minute before rolling over for her morning belly rub. Never ceases to make me start the day with a smile!

"While I will never know Bess's backstory of her first seven months before she was picked up as a malnour-ished stray," Debbie added, "I do know she is safe now and I will always protect her, and I'm pretty sure she's got my back, too."

For Adrienne Finney, keeper of the Guilford Gang, the days are filled with wonderful moments captured in thousands of pictures. The dogs have the run of the magnificent Vermont farm where they live almost all day, every day. As I said, it's doggy heaven. Because they get so much exercise, they are usually tired by the time Adrienne finally sits down to watch a little TV in the evening.

"I don't watch a lot of TV, but when I do the dogs are all in the room with me," Adrienne told me. "Some are

---

*Shortly after these words were written in October 2016 Tucker was diagnosed with cancer, but was doing well at last word.

sitting in chairs, or with me on the floor, and others are scattered all around me just lying there. I can sense their peace and comfort. We're just a big puppy pile here. I love these moments when they are just with me and all is quiet and I can really experience them by reaching out and petting them and they don't even raise their heads because they're so tired. It's so calm and comfortable."

"My favorite time of day is when I am going up to bed and Bart is just coming in from his walk," Amy Lovett told me. "When he sees me going upstairs he gets so happy because he's allowed in the bed. He turns himself around on the bed, puts his head on my ankles, and lets out a big sigh, as if to say, *We're done for the day. Let's go to sleep*. At night, once the kids are in bed it's just the two of us; or the three of us, if you count my husband! Knowing he's there is relaxing. It could have been the hardest day at work, but he tells me it's done and not to worry. We can pick it up tomorrow.

"I also love coming home to Bart," Amy said. "He's always at the door when I come home, so it's Bart and the kids all coming at me together."

THE GREETING UPON COMING HOME was a recurring moment most folks identified as special in their lives with their dogs. Andrea Stewart told me that when she walks in the door in the evening after work, Linda is often there sitting in her favorite chair. Before she knows it, Noah bursts forth at her "like the creature from *Alien*," but all giddy and excited. And, as we saw earlier, Noah treasures every piece of attention Linda gives him, even having his nails clipped and his teeth brushed, which many dogs can hardly tolerate. Such ordinary, pedestrian moments in our lives, but such special ones, too.

The importance of holding on to the memories of the small moments and appreciating them while they last was driven home for me by Elissa Altman of Newtown, Connecticut. Living in a community that has experienced a shocking, indescribable loss where dozens of parents, teachers, first responders, and everyone else are living with overwhelming memories of the moments large and small that comprised the lives of those who were lost probably makes you all the more attentive to how fleeting precious moments can be.

"I work at home," Elissa told me, "and Susan works in the city. Unless I was in the throes of writing a book, I stopped work about five p.m. or five thirty p.m. I'd pour a glass of wine and sit on the front stoop with Addie on one side of me and Petey on the other. When she got old Addie could barely jog, but both of them would jump to their feet to greet Susan when she came home from work. The first day without Addie, Petey was still excited, but it was very different. I miss that."

———

THE MORE ORDINARY these moments with our loved ones (human, canine, or otherwise), the more we will miss them and cherish them when they cease to exist. And each one is like one of those eggs in Woody Allen's monologue. Despite years of picking up poop in plastic bags, cleaning up the accidents in the house, and the dirt and the mud and an occasional small animal dragged into the house, despite the frozen early morning walks in February, the seemingly endless trips to the vet, the expressed anal glands, the torn-up gardens and occasionally chewed-up bedspreads, despite the barking and the whining, the begging at the dinner table, and the shed fur that clings to clothes and carpets and car seats, notwithstanding the sometimes sleepless nights, the injuries, and the eventual grief, we continue to search for these dogs, save them from dire fates, bring them to live with us as family members in our homes, and love them until death do us part.

As for Albie and me, we're still walking the woods on autumn afternoons and watching the seasons change together. Sometimes our relationships with our dogs are totally crazy and absurd, but I guess we keep going through it because, for all the early mornings and sleepless nights, poop piles and muddy paws, most of us need the love, the affirmation, and all the joy they bring us. In other words, we need the eggs.

Epilogue

*If there are no dogs in Heaven, then when I die I want
to go where they went.* —Will Rogers

*Jamba, the newest addition
to the Zheutlin gang, with
Salina and Albie.*

Shortly before finalizing the manuscript for this book, I checked in with many of the people I had interviewed to see what, if anything, was new in their lives with their dogs. Others had written me with updates.

In December of 2016 I received an e-mail from Ericka Kofkin, the young deaf woman from Florida who adopted Zosia, the pit bull found by railroad tracks with both of her hind legs severed. Ericka's e-mail reminded me that there are times that are so tough it is in the dog's best interest to be placed in another home. Ericka became seriously ill and was no longer able to care for Zosia. Most good rescues will ask that you return the dog to them in such circumstances, and Zosia did go back into foster care with the Pit Sisters. Responsible rescues don't want the dog to go just anywhere and their commitment to the dogs they save is for a lifetime; they want to be sure each dog finds another excellent home, as Ericka's was while she was well. Ericka told me parting with Zosia was "devastating." But the story has a happy ending. In late February 2017, Zosia found a new home with a Jacksonville family that fell head over heels in love with her.

Elissa Altman, the writer from Newtown, Connecticut, wrote and told me that Petey, who had missed their other rescue dog Addie so much when she died, had been diagnosed with soft-tissue sarcoma on one of his toes. The cancer was removed but it's likely, Elissa wrote, that he'll need to have that toe amputated in the next few months. Without Addie, Petey "has grown much more attached to us," wrote Elissa, "more affectionate and he's doing well. We pray for his health every day. And every day, I look around the house for Addie and whisper, 'Where are you?'"

Staicey Scholtz, who, with her husband, Brad, welcomed Jacob ("Jake") into their home for his final few months after a life of deprivation, wrote that they think of him every day even though he's been gone five years.

"We have a corner of a dollar bill tacked up on our message board that makes us smile and think about the time we came home to dollar bills shredded all over the living room. That money destroying episode might have cost us $17, but the memory is priceless.

"He really was a 'train wreck' when we adopted him," Staicey continued, "but something about all the stresses and rigors of teaching him about home life reaffirmed to us that dogs are amazingly forgiving and don't live in the past. Every day of his short eight-month life in his forever home, he woke up in a warm plush bed with a mom and dad that loved him. He repaid us in many ways—from rolling on his back with happy grunts each and every morning to mastering the 'sit' and 'down' commands. When we opened the front door to greet our friends and family he no longer bolted away. I think he finally knew he was HOME.

"Jacob inspired my husband to never doubt adopting an older dog," Staicey concluded. "We are currently raising our seventh assistance dog as volunteer puppy raisers for Canine Companions for Independence and look for our next 'Big Jake' to touch our lives."

Nancy Allen-Ziemski, the prolific fosterer from Norwich, Connecticut, wrote to say that her Rosco, who celebrated his seventh Gotcha Day in late January, was joined by Ellie, a young Lab surrendered by her family to a high-kill shelter in Louisiana. Ellie and Rosco love to swim in the pool together.

Young Teagan Sparhawk gave up Christmas presents and instead created twenty-five gift bags with assorted dog goodies (leashes, collars, and treats) that she donated, along with food and blankets, to a local shelter. Her father, Brian, wrote me that in 2016 Teagan donated more than $10,000 in cash and goods to various rescue organizations, and they are working with a lawyer to explore the possibility of creating their own nonprofit organization to support other rescue groups. "Teagan will be ten this year," Brian wrote, "and we are encouraging her to take an even more active role in rescuing and advocating . . . Her passion is not waning."

Heather Fuqua of Pineville, Louisiana, added another rescue to her brood, Rocky, a six-year-old purebred border collie. "He is just as awesome as my other rescues," Heather wrote. "My daughter showed him in the open 4H show for dogs and they won first place and best in show! Rescue is the way to go!"

Sixty-five-year-old Joanne Sebring of Stroudsburg, Pennsylvania—"mom" to Trace, Roxy, Ziggy, and Buddy—took a job as a receptionist at a veterinarian's office, "to help pay for dog food!" she wrote, and added a new rescue, Quincy, to the brood. Quincy is a one-year-old deaf English setter. "He's my biggest challenge ever," wrote Joanne, "because along with his deafness he also has some OCD such as continually chasing and barking at shadows. He's as sweet as can be and very smart. He's learned and responds to a variety of hand signals I've taught him. The trick is catching his eye so he sees them!"

Kelly Thompson of Branford, Connecticut, who, with her husband, Greg, adopted Estelle and then went through heartbreak when they learned she had a fatal heart affliction related to heartworm disease, adopted another yellow Lab from Louisiana named Winnie. "We think Estelle sent her to us as she has some of the same characteristics," Kelly wrote.

In late January, just before the Super Bowl, ABC's *Good Morning America* launched its "Pawdoption Bowl," sending NFL stars to shelters across the country to encourage people to adopt rescue dogs. Not surprisingly, Ronnie Stanley, who had a successful rookie year with the Baltimore Ravens, kicked off the event. "I asked for the most unadoptable pet, pretty much," Ronnie told ABC, referring to Lola. "If you're thinking about getting a dog, definitely go to the shelter first," he added. "I think rescue dogs are more appreciative." Through the Ravens publicity office Ronnie let me know that Lola was doing great and that all was well.

Amy Lovett of Troy, New York, wrote to say that Guinness turned sixteen in December and "is still going. The last time it snowed she was like a puppy in the snow. She's still our 'guard dog,' seemingly sound asleep until someone jogs by or a deer wanders into the yard, and then she's at the front window protecting her home and her family with her deep bark." Bart gained some weight from the enforced inactivity required when undergoing a second heartworm treatment, but he now has a clean bill of health and is off the heartworm medication.

And, finally, I caught up with Jason Bertrand, the Florida inmate who adopted Sugar Mama, the dog he trained in prison. He was released just before Christmas 2016, having spent roughly half his life behind bars. Shortly thereafter he reconnected with Crystal Miller, a girl he'd gone to school with at age fourteen, and they fell in love.

The original plan was for Sugar Mama to be fostered for a while as Jason got settled into his new life, but that changed and they've been together throughout. Jason, Crystal, Sugar Mama, and Emma, Crystal's Jack Russell terrier, are living together in a rented house in New Port Richey, Florida. Jason found a job a few weeks after his release at Office Depot with a regular salary and plans in his spare time to begin a one-year apprenticeship at a Pinellas County tattoo parlor run by a friend he met in prison, a prerequisite for opening his own parlor.

"Sugar Mama has been very important to me during this transition," Jason told me by phone. "She helps me to be responsible. I have to take care of her. I can't stay out all hours because I have to be home for her."

Tackling new technology has been one of Jason's biggest challenges, but simply adapting to life on the outside has been "a huge adjustment." Same for Sugar

Mama. "She was afraid of a lot of things at first," said Jason. "Even the magnets on the refrigerator scared her. She was also used to being locked up and confined."

Despite the challenges, Jason says he is optimistic about the future he is walking toward, with Sugar Mama, ever faithful, by his side.

As for Judy and me, in the early summer of 2016 we welcomed a third rescue dog from Louisiana into our home. Like Albie and Salina, she was one of the many dogs Keri Toth saves every year, and like Albie and Salina, she came north with Greg Mahle's Rescue Road Trips.

Jambalaya, or Jamba, for short, is the name our older son Danny gave her, a nod to her Louisiana roots. She's Danny's dog, but since he lives in an apartment in downtown Boston and is just starting his career, she lives with us most of the time. Jamba is a small black Lab mix, only about forty pounds. She appears to have some pointer and hound in her. She's about two years old and had already been a mama by the time she came to us.

She made herself at home right away. She and Salina, perhaps because they are the two girls, love to mix it up, and one of Jamba's favorite maneuvers, because Salina stands a bit taller than she does, is to walk right under Salina's belly and essentially get Salina straddled over her small black body and thus immobilized. To free herself takes quite a bit of wriggling on Salina's part. Except for some occasional food aggression, Albie has accepted

Jamba with aplomb. Jamba quickly asserted herself in our bed at night, occasionally joined by one or both of the others, which makes for some contorted sleeping positions, to say the least. Mostly, however, Salina claimed the guest room bed and Albie sometimes sleeps in a dog bed meant for Jamba on the floor of our bedroom, one far too small for his eighty-pound body but which he really seems to like. But most nights he crawls under our bed, much as he slept under the coffee table in our living room when he first came to us.

In some ways having three isn't much more work than having two, but there are times when I think we are pushing our limit. When the wild turkeys appear in our yard and all three are barking at them, the Tower of Babel can be overwhelming. Albie has a deep, husky bark, Salina one in the mid-range, but Jamba—well, perhaps because of her size, hers is shrill, sharp, and ear-splitting. I don't love all the barking, but I love each of the dogs.

Jamba is unusually affectionate and craves human touch. If you pet her she won't just stand or sit there, she'll lean into you with all her weight. And compared with the sometimes neurotic Albie, and the slightly aloof Salina, she seems to exist in a perpetual state of joy and wonderment and delight.

As the autumn leaves started to fall in October and into November, Jamba would be out in the backyard scanning the trees back and forth, waiting for the next leaf to drop. Then she'd launch herself full-tilt at every one to try and catch it before it hit the ground. In early fall there were only a couple of leaves every few minutes, but she concentrated intently, turning her head this way and that to try to spy a floating leaf. As the season progressed, especially on breezy days, the leaves would come down in droves, and she ran every which way trying to catch as many as she could, overwhelmed by the target-rich environment. Neither Albie nor Salina shows any interest in falling leaves. But watching Jamba, sometimes from the house while she was alone outside, running and leaping and giving each leaf she caught a good shake before dropping it so she could pursue another, was great entertainment. She was completely lost in her own reverie. It reminded me of a small child chasing hundreds of bubbles, lost in a magical world of wonder, utterly in the moment and utterly joyful.

It's not only leaves she loves to pursue. She never, ever tires of having a tennis ball thrown to her, either. She chases it with such exuberance, she often overruns it, her back legs furiously trying to grip the turf so she can stop, turn, and get the ball and bring it back. Sometimes she stops so suddenly she completely flips over. She also loves Frisbees, though her preferred activity with a Frisbee is to take it in her mouth and run full-tilt back and forth across the lawn with the Frisbee upside down in her mouth. At the end of each half lap, when she reaches the edge of the yard, she vigorously shakes her head left and right and growls as if she's trying to teach the stupid Frisbee a lesson or, perhaps, disembowel it.

There's one other little habit of hers that I love. When we let the dogs into the backyard they have to run across the deck to a set of four steps that leads down to the lawn. Albie and Salina take each step, but Jamba has her own unique way of getting to the lawn. She launches herself from the deck, flies over the steps, and lands on all fours on the grass, her ears spread out like little wings from the undercurrent. It's the way most dogs jump into a pool. There's something about that little maneuver that seems to capture her joie de vivre.

We've fallen in love yet again. But now I have a big decision to make. Do I refer to myself as her granddaddy? Or would that be a little much?

Acknowledgments

FIRST AND FOREMOST, my gratitude goes to everyone who shared his or her rescue story with me for this book. I won't repeat their names here because all are mentioned, most multiple times, in the text. It's a testament to the unique and powerful bond between people and their rescue dogs that people are so eager to share their stories and to pay tribute to the dogs that have reciprocated their love many times over. What makes the entire rescue movement so emotionally powerful is that it so often begins in tragedy but ends in love, at least for the lucky few, relatively speaking, who escape the streets and high-kill shelters. And I want to thank everyone out there, those whose names I know and those I don't, who do their part for dogs like Albie, Salina, and Jambalaya, and the others you've met in this book.

Stephanie Bowen, my thoughtful and compassionate editor for *Rescue Road* when she worked at Sourcebooks, was also my editor for this book in her new job at TarcherPerigee. She flatters me, or more precisely my writing, enough to make me think I might actually be a pretty decent writer. I am grateful to Stephanie for her continued confidence in me and for her many contributions to this book. The job of a good editor is to make the writer appear better than he or she is, and Stephanie is very good at her job.

Thank you as well to the production, design, and publicity teams at TarcherPerigee (especially Jennifer Tait in managing editorial, Katy Riegel in design, Jessica Morphew in the cover department, and Keely Platte and Brianna Yamashita in publicity), for all your work to make this book a reality. Thank you also to Dave Cole for copy editing.

This is the sixth book I have worked on with my agent Joelle Delbourgo, who I also now consider a friend. My thanks to Joelle for her ongoing support and advice and belief in me.

My wife, Judy, is the generator of most of the good ideas I have turned into articles and books. Some of those books I've written alone and a couple we've written together. She's the spark I sometimes need to get my rear in gear and stop mulling an idea and start acting on it. My sons, Danny and Noah, are both wonderful young men whom I love very much and I thank them just for being themselves.

Thanks to Tom Valente of the Baltimore Ravens for facilitating my conversation with Ronnie Stanley.

My author photograph was taken by Chip Fanelli who passed away in early 2017 after a long battle with ALS. Chip was a wonderful guy and a talented photographer who left us way too young.

And finally, thanks to Albie, Salina, and Jambalaya; Noah (the shaggy dog); Noelle; Tucker; Thabiso; Guinness; the Guilford Gang; and all the other underdogs whose names and stories appear in these pages. Every one of these stories is much-needed inspiration in an often unkind and unjust world.

Illustration Credits

Dedication: Courtesy of the author

Introduction: Courtesy of the author

Chapter 1: Andrea Stewart

Chapter 2: Staicey Scholtz

Chapter 3: Nancy Allen-Ziemski

Chapter 4: Ericka Kofkin

Chapter 5: Brian Sparhawk

Chapter 6: Heather Fuqua

Chapter 7: Craig O'Neal

Chapter 8: Allison Smith

Chapter 9: Doreen Dawson

Chapter 10: Allison Smith

Chapter 11: Adrienne Finney

Epilogue: Emily Okun

CHIP FANELLI

ABOUT THE AUTHOR

PETER ZHEUTLIN is a freelance journalist and author whose work has appeared regularly in *The Boston Globe* and *The Christian Science Monitor*. He has also written for the *Los Angeles Times, Parade* magazine, *AARP the Magazine*, and numerous other publications in the United States and abroad. Zheutlin is the author of *New York Times* bestseller *Rescue Road: One Man, Thirty Thousand Dogs, and a Million Miles on the Last Hope Highway* and *Around the World on Two Wheels: Annie Londonderry's Extraordinary Ride*. He is also the coauthor, with Thomas B. Graboys, MD, of *Life in the Balance: A Physician's Memoir of Life, Love, and Loss with Parkinson's Disease and Dementia*; with Robert P. Smith, of *Riches Among the Ruins: Adventures in the Dark Corners of the Global Economy*; and, with Judith Gelman, of

The Unofficial Mad Men Cookbook: Inside the Kitchens, Bars, and Restaurants of Mad Men and *The Unofficial Girls Guide to New York: Inside the Cafés, Clubs, and Neighborhoods of HBO's Girls*. He is a graduate of Amherst College and Boston College Law School and resides in Massachusetts with his wife, author Judith Gelman. He has two grown sons and three rescue dogs.